MISSION ALIGNED. DATA DRIVEN.
A PRACTICAL FRAMEWORK FOR CULTIVATING A CULTURE OF EXCELLENCE IN NONPROFIT ORGANIZATIONS

TERRY "SHAWN" HOWELL

CONTENTS

Foreword	vii
1. THE PURSUIT OF EXCELLENCE	1
What is Excellence?	1
Why Excellence Matters	3
The Challenge of Pursuing Excellence	5
Final Thoughts	7
Reflection	8
2. THE FOUR MENTALITIES	9
A Question That Changed Everything	9
The Compliance Mentality	11
The Service Mentality	13
The Results Mentality	14
The Mission Aligned Data Driven Mentality	15
Final Thoughts	17
Reflection	18
3. THE FRAMEWORK	19
Turning Insights into Action	19
Results Oriented Management and Accountability	20
CSBG Organizational Standards	21
CSBG Standards of Excellence	21
Building On The Foundation	22
The INSPIRE Framework	35
Final Thoughts	38
Reflection	39
4. GETTING STARTED	41
Laying the Foundation for Success	41
The INSPIRE Committee	42
Balancing Time, Skills, and Resources	43
Final Thoughts	46
Reflection	47

5. IDENTITY — 49
- A Strong Foundation — 49
- Listening to the Voices of the Team — 51
- Defining the Problem — 52
- A Vision for the Future — 57
- The Mission: Defining the Purpose — 60
- Values and Beliefs: The Heart of the Organization — 67
- Goals: Expanding the Mission — 71
- Final Thoughts — 75
- Reflection — 76

6. NAVIGATION — 77
- Understanding the Landscape — 77
- Data: The Foundation for Identifying Barriers — 80
- The Community Assessment: Understanding External Factors — 88
- Organizational Assessment: Evaluating Internal Factors — 97
- Final Thoughts — 106
- Reflection — 107

7. STRATEGY — 109
- Strategy as the Pinnacle of INSPIRE — 109
- Preparation — 114
- The Planning Session — 114
- Finalizing and Presenting the Strategic Plan — 131
- Board Review and Approval — 132
- Ongoing Monitoring and Accountability — 132
- Final Thoughts — 134
- Reflection — 135

8. PERFORMANCE — 137
- Where Preparation Meets the Moment — 137
- Stay on Target — 138
- Creating Feedback Loops — 141
- Tracking the Right Data — 142
- Course Correction and Continuous Improvement — 144
- Sustaining Performance Through Mental Wellness — 146
- Celebrating Wins — 148
- Final Thoughts — 150
- Reflection — 151

9. INSPECTION ... 153
  From Information to Insight ... 153
  Why Inspection Matters ... 154
  The Importance of Data Quality ... 155
  Types of Analysis ... 156
  Making Analysis Simple ... 160
  Digging Deeper Into Performance Accuracy ... 176
  What the Numbers Reveal ... 179
  Final Thoughts ... 184
  Reflection ... 185

10. REPORTING ... 187
  Reframing Reporting as Strategic Communication ... 187
  Who Was Wilbur Schramm? ... 188
  Schramm's Model of Communication ... 189
  Moving from Theory to Action ... 191
  Navigating Noise ... 205
  Building Feedback Loops ... 207
  Final Thoughts ... 209
  Reflection ... 211

11. ENRICHMENT ... 213
  The Journey Has No Finish Line ... 213
  Why Continuous Improvement Matters ... 215
  Culture as the Engine of Improvement ... 216
  Building Blocks of Continuous Improvement ... 219
  Leading the Culture ... 227
  Staying in Motion ... 229
  Final Thoughts ... 231
  Reflection ... 232

12. LEADERSHIP COMMITMENT ... 233
  Leading the Way Forward ... 233

  Notes ... 237
  About the Author ... 241

FOREWORD

I grew up knowing what it feels like to stand on the outside looking in—to be the kid not picked for the team, to live with the quiet, heavy weight that poverty places on a child's shoulders. Poverty isolates. It builds walls around dreams, opportunities, even dignity. And once you've lived inside those walls, you never forget them.

But I also learned that walls can be torn down. The work of tearing them down—of restoring dignity, opportunity, and hope—is some of the most important work anyone can do for themselves and those around them.

Community Action came into my life early—as a Head Start student, the son of a Head Start teacher, and later as an employee within the network. Through it, I discovered something powerful: when mission is aligned with action, and action is aligned with real impact, we don't just change individual lives—we change communities.

When I transitioned to consulting in 2017, I began working with a broader range of nonprofits and mission-driven organizations.

FOREWORD

It was at this point I learned that while the challenges varied, the heart of the work remained the same.

Wherever true impact was happening, it was because leaders were committed to more than just good intentions. They were committed to excellence. To data. To truth-telling. To doing the hard work of getting better every day.

That's what this book is about. It's a culmination of the lessons I've learned—a way to give back to the mission that has given so much to me. It's my hope that other children won't have to grow up behind the same walls I once knew, that communities will be strengthened, that meaningful employment, dignity, and hope can be available to all. That together, we can live out the calling to help others—not with pity, but with partnership, and with a commitment to real, lasting change.

We are living in a time when this work has never been more urgent. Programs are under attack, resources are shrinking, and public conversations are growing harsher. But even in the face of those realities, I believe something even stronger: we can make a difference.

And you don't have to do it alone.

As you read this book, I hope you will be inspired to think differently and equipped to act differently—with your mission in mind, your data in hand, and your heart fully engaged. I hope you will see that excellence is not reserved for the privileged few; it's built, day by day, choice by choice, by those who refuse to accept "good enough" when the mission demands excellence.

You are not alone.

You are part of something bigger than yourself—something bold, courageous, and necessary.

So let's move forward together—stronger, smarter, and more determined than ever. Let's build organizations worthy of the missions we serve. Let's do it together.

CHAPTER 1
THE PURSUIT OF EXCELLENCE

WHAT IS EXCELLENCE?

Excellence. It's a term proudly included in mission statements, boardroom discussions, and grant proposals. It often appears in the titles of awards, promoted as the standard of achievement that nearly every organization aspires to.

The *Oxford English Dictionary* defines excellence as "the quality of being outstanding or extremely good."[1] While this definition sounds straightforward, terms like *outstanding* and *extremely good* can be subjective and open to interpretation. Without a shared understanding, organizations often fall into the trap of superficial indicators: flawless audits, steady funding, or the absence of mistakes. These markers may provide stability, but they fail to capture the transformative power of true excellence. Rather than focusing on a fixed definition, this book invites you to explore what excellence really means in practice—through stories, questions, and frameworks that challenge assumptions and provoke deeper thinking. By the end, you may find that excellence isn't something to be defined, but something to be lived.

Excellence has always been more than a goal—it's a guiding principle that defines how we approach our work and our lives. As a child, my father often reminded me, *"Do your work as unto the Lord,"* a principle that instilled in me the importance of giving my best, no matter the circumstances. This mentality shaped how I view success—not as a measure of power or wealth, but as the intentional effort to create meaningful change. For organizations, the pursuit of excellence demands the same intentionality: to look beyond surface-level achievements and align every effort with a greater purpose.

"Excellence isn't something to be defined, but something to be lived"

As an example, I want to introduce you to my friend Matt. Matt works for a successful production company in my area that often serves highly prestigious customers. On one occasion, there was an issue balancing one of the cameras being prepared for a show. While someone recommended using a sandbag, Matt went beyond the call of duty to make sure the company maintained an appearance of professionalism that matched the services they provided. He purchased a weight from a local sporting goods store, removed the handle with a saw, and then welded bolts into the weights that would screw into the front of the tripod, ensuring the camera

THE PURSUIT OF EXCELLENCE

could be easily balanced, even when outfitted with a lightweight lens. His actions were an excellent example of going the extra mile—not just solving a problem but doing so in a way that elevated the company's standards and strengthened its reputation.

Matt's custom camera weight—repurposed and precision-welded to balance professional equipment—demonstrates his personal commitment to excellence.

Matt's actions remind us that excellence requires resourcefulness and a willingness to go beyond conventional solutions. Nonprofits face similar challenges, where limited resources and high stakes demand both creativity and a steadfast commitment to purpose. Unexpected challenges can make it tempting to take shortcuts, but true excellence demands intentionality and creativity. It means proactively seeking better ways to serve, even when no one is watching, and choosing impact over convenience. Excellence requires organizations to reflect honestly on their work, acknowledge areas for growth, and have the courage to adapt when needed. It's a mindset—a continuous journey of purpose-driven action that transforms lives, strengthens communities, and ensures that every effort contributes to meaningful change.

WHY EXCELLENCE MATTERS

The nonprofit sector in the United States is vast, with nearly 2 million organizations addressing critical societal challenges such as poverty, hunger, education, and healthcare. While each cause is important, competition for resources is fierce, and government funding is becoming increasingly difficult to secure. In this environment, adequacy may keep an organization running, but it won't inspire the confidence, trust, or investment needed to thrive.

Funders—whether individuals, foundations, or government agencies—are looking for more than an organization that serves a few people each year with basic needs. They seek bold solutions that create measurable outcomes and address root causes. Organizations that go beyond meeting expectations to embrace innovation and pursue transformative results stand out in the crowded landscape. Whether piloting new programs to reduce homelessness or leveraging technology to increase efficiency, excellence captures the attention of funders and builds trust by demonstrating a steadfast commitment to meaningful change.

"Adequacy may keep an organization running, but it won't inspire trust, investment, or transformation."

Excellence also fosters collaboration. When stakeholders recognize an organization's dedication to purpose-driven outcomes, they are more willing to engage as true partners, contributing resources, expertise, and ideas. Trust built on a foundation of excellence changes these partnerships from transactional to transformational, amplifying the collective ability to address pressing issues and achieve lasting results.

Internally, excellence inspires momentum. It empowers staff and volunteers to take pride in their work, encouraging creativity, collaboration, and a sense of ownership. When an organization embraces excellence as a standard, it unites teams around a shared mission, cultivating a culture where every effort feels purposeful and impactful.

THE CHALLENGE OF PURSUING EXCELLENCE

The pursuit of excellence is as demanding as it is rewarding. It calls for courage to challenge the status quo, a willingness to embrace change, and a steadfast focus on long-term impact over short-term convenience. For many organizations, the fear of failure becomes a barrier, leading them to cling to familiar processes or safe decisions. Yet, excellence is found not in avoiding failure but in learning from it, using setbacks as opportunities to innovate and adapt.

Moving beyond comfort zones is essential. Comfort often reinforces habits and processes that, while reliable, are outdated and inefficient. Excellence requires bold leadership willing to step into the unknown, experiment with new approaches, and ask difficult questions. A strong vision for the future, supported by a dedicated team and a collaborative spirit, becomes the foundation for driving meaningful progress.

Collaboration, both internally and externally, is a critical aspect of this journey. Internally, it means fostering an environment where staff and volunteers feel empowered to contribute creatively and work toward shared goals across departmental lines. Externally, it involves building partnerships with other organizations, funders, and stakeholders who share a commitment to achieving purpose-driven outcomes. Together, these relationships create the synergy necessary to address complex challenges and amplify impact.

Excellence is not a milestone or a destination; it is a continuous journey, defined by intentional reflection and deliberate action. Leaders must maintain clarity of purpose, align their strategies with the organization's mission, and ensure that progress is celebrated along the way. Incremental successes fuel momentum, while a commitment to adaptability ensures resilience in the face of challenges.

This book serves as a guide to help organizations understand what drives excellence and establish a framework for fostering a culture that continually strives for it. The journey isn't about arriving at a place of perfection but about cultivating a mentality that thrives on continuous improvement, meaningful collaboration, and transformative results.

FINAL THOUGHTS

Excellence isn't simply about avoiding mistakes or meeting expectations; it's about creating meaningful change that aligns with your mission and transforms lives. It's a relentless dedication to purpose-driven growth, innovation, and empowerment. This journey starts by challenging assumptions, aligning actions with values, and embracing the courage to aim higher.

In the next chapter, we'll explore the mentalities that shape how organizations define success. These insights will help you break free from limitations and move closer to cultivating a culture of excellence

REFLECTION

Understanding your organization's culture and approach to excellence requires intentional reflection. Excellence is not a destination but a continuous journey, shaped by how your organization defines, communicates, and pursues its purpose. These questions will help you evaluate your current practices and identify opportunities to foster a culture of continuous improvement.

- **Assess:** *How does your organization define excellence, and is this definition consistently communicated and understood across all levels?*

- **Reflect:** *In what ways could fear of failure, resistance to change, or outdated processes hold your organization back from pursuing excellence?*

- **Act:** *What is one step your organization can take today to build a culture of excellence and continuous improvement?*

CHAPTER 2
THE FOUR MENTALITIES

A QUESTION THAT CHANGED EVERYTHING

It was the fall of 2017, and I was attending a continuing education class in Seattle, Washington. We had a packed schedule, but the sessions were engaging and productive for maintaining our professional certifications. During a short break, I stepped away to clear my head when a colleague caught up with me in the hallway. He didn't waste time with small talk. Instead, he asked a single, unassuming question: *"Do you think they are getting it?"*

I knew exactly what he meant. He wanted to know if I thought the organizations we worked with—and even some certified professionals in the room—truly understood what it meant to be results-oriented and accountable.

I paused, reflecting on the organizations I had served during the past year. These were nonprofits filled with passionate, hardworking individuals—often stretched thin by limited resources and growing demands. Many were doing their best to stay compliant, but did they truly embrace the concepts we were teaching? Finally, I replied, *"No. I think most are just going through the motions."*

He nodded in agreement, and we stood there for a moment in silence, both lost in thought about what that meant before returning to our seats.

It wasn't just about the organizations I served. It was about the systems, assumptions, and mentalities shaping how they operated. It forced me to confront a critical issue: the connection between how organizations define success and their pursuit of excellence.

For years, I had worked at an organization widely regarded as one of the best in the industry. We had built nationally recognized programs and cultivated a culture where success was measured through the impact of our work.

Yet, in my consulting work, I saw something very different. Many organizations weren't even sure how to measure success. Instead, they relied on what felt right: outputs counted, deadlines met, and funder expectations satisfied. But if you don't understand success, how can you ever pursue excellence?

That conversation made me ask a deeper question: How do organizations define success, and do they define it in a way that supports excellence? As I explored this further, I began to notice patterns in how organizations approached success. Through organizational assessments, consultations, and candid conversations with leaders, it became clear that the measurement of success generally fell into one of four categories—or mentalities. These mentalities represented the culture of the entity and shaped not only their definitions of success but also their ability—or inability—to pursue true excellence.

THE FOUR MENTALITIES

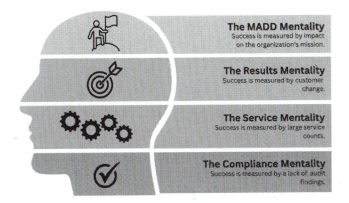

Understanding these mentalities became the foundation for uncovering what holds organizations back and what allows them to thrive. Each mentality offered a window into how organizations understood their purpose, measured their impact, and pursued their goals. Some created environments where excellence could thrive. Others built walls that made it nearly impossible.

THE COMPLIANCE MENTALITY

The Compliance Mentality is one of the most prevalent mindsets I've encountered, particularly in organizations reliant on government grants or heavily regulated funding streams. At first glance, compliance seems practical—even responsible. It ensures organizations meet their obligations to funders and maintain operational stability. However, compliance doesn't make you good, it just makes you legal.

Organizations in this mindset often define success by the absence of problems. Reports are submitted on time, audits are passed, and grant conditions are fulfilled. These achievements are necessary for survival, but they represent the bare minimum. Compliance ensures an organization keeps its doors open, but it rarely drives meaningful growth or innovation.

I once evaluated an organization's strategic plan that epitomized this mentality. The plan offered little forward-looking vision or innovation. Instead, it reflected on the past year and culminated in a single goal: to maintain CSBG (Community Services Block Grant) funding. That was it. There were no aspirational hopes, no strategies for greater impact—just a focus on keeping the money flowing. While this goal ensured short-term survival, it underscored the stagnation that defines the Compliance Mentality.

This mindset often stems from fear. Organizations fear losing funding, making mistakes, or drawing the wrong kind of attention. While these concerns provide a sense of security, they also create walls that stifle creativity and limit the ability to pursue transformative change. Over time, these walls become a cage, trapping leaders and staff in a cycle of doing just enough to avoid problems, rather than striving to achieve their mission.

"Compliance doesn't make you good, it just makes you legal."

Perhaps the greatest risk of the Compliance Mentality is its tendency to prioritize process over purpose. Staff become adept at navigating requirements and avoiding penalties, but the organization's mission takes a backseat. Over time, the relentless pursuit of playing it safe obscures the purpose that should drive every decision and action.

Breaking free from the Compliance Mentality requires a fundamental shift in perspective. Compliance should not be viewed as the ultimate goal but as a foundation for pursuing something greater. Leaders must challenge themselves to move beyond simply meeting standards and instead ask, *"How can compliance support, rather than constrain, our efforts to fulfill our mission?"*

THE SERVICE MENTALITY

The Service Mentality is characterized by a focus on volume—the number of clients served, or services delivered—without fully evaluating the impact of those efforts. This approach is common among organizations providing emergency services, such as food pantries or utility assistance programs. While this mindset often stems from a genuine desire to help as many people as possible, it can create significant issues when quantity is prioritized over quality and effectiveness.

Consider the operations of many food pantries. These organizations often report the total number of meals provided on a weekly or monthly basis. However, as the same individuals return for services week after week, the numbers accumulate over time. At the end of the year, these duplicated counts are often reported as the number of "people served." In some cases, the reported figures exceed not only the number of food-insecure individuals in the area, but even the total population of the community. This inflation undermines the organization's credibility and can damage trust with funders, stakeholders, and the public.

The Service Mentality values action for its own sake. Leaders and boards frequently equate busyness with success, celebrating packed schedules or high activity levels as proof of impact. However, when the data is examined, it often reveals that the organization's efforts lack alignment with community needs or long-term sustainability. Instead of addressing root causes or driving systemic change, resources are spread thin across activities that may yield minimal results.

This mentality also takes a toll on staff and volunteers. Organizations driven by the Service Mentality often overextend their teams, leading to long hours, overlapping responsibilities, and high levels of stress. Over time, this can create a culture of burnout. Staff members become disengaged, morale declines, and turnover increases. The resulting exhaustion limits the organization's capacity to sustain its work and fulfill its mission.

To move beyond the Service Mentality, organizations must shift their focus from busyness to intentionality. This requires examining whether their efforts align with their mission and address the true needs of the community. It also means valuing the well-being of staff and volunteers, creating a culture that prioritizes impact over sheer activity. By doing so, organizations can break free from the cycle of burnout and ensure that every action contributes to meaningful and lasting change.

THE RESULTS MENTALITY

The Results Mentality marks a significant improvement over the Compliance and Service Mentalities by prioritizing measurable outcomes. Organizations in this mindset seek to demonstrate that their work produces tangible, positive change. This focus on accountability and progress is a step forward, but it often falls short in one critical area: alignment.

THE FOUR MENTALITIES

Outcomes are measured, but they frequently lack connection to the organization's overarching mission. Programs operate in silos, data systems are fragmented, and leaders struggle to articulate a cohesive narrative about the organization's overall impact. This disconnection isn't just an operational challenge—it actively undermines the ability to inspire confidence among stakeholders.

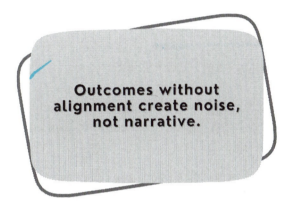

Outcomes without alignment create noise, not narrative.

True excellence requires more than measurable outcomes—it demands intentional alignment. By integrating data, connecting programs, and ensuring that every action supports the mission, organizations can transform fragmented efforts into a compelling story of systemic change. This alignment not only strengthens the organization's narrative but also enables it to achieve a deeper and more sustainable impact.

THE MISSION ALIGNED DATA DRIVEN MENTALITY

The Mission Aligned Data Driven (MADD) Mentality represents the pinnacle of organizational thinking, combining the strengths of Compliance, Service, and Results while addressing their shortcomings. At its core, MADD is defined by two principles:

15

mission alignment and a passionate reliance on data to drive decisions.

Unlike other mentalities, MADD fosters connection. It integrates systems, breaks down silos, and ensures that every program and policy aligns with the organization's mission. This unified approach enables organizations to measure their impact holistically, tell a cohesive story of transformation, and build trust with stakeholders.

MADD is not about tracking what's easy to measure but about focusing on what matters most. It requires organizations to ask hard questions about whether their efforts are truly fulfilling their mission and creating sustainable change. By aligning data, programs, and purpose, MADD transforms organizations from reactive to proactive, from fragmented to unified, and from merely surviving to thriving.

This mentality demands courage, discipline, and visionary leadership. Adopting MADD involves stepping away from the familiar and committing to a culture of intentionality, collaboration, and purpose-driven excellence. For organizations willing to take this step, the rewards are profound: sustainable impact, empowered teams, and enduring trust within the community.

In the chapters ahead, we'll explore how to bring the MADD Mentality to life in your organization, aligning your mission, connecting your data, and fostering a culture of purpose-driven excellence.

FINAL THOUGHTS

The Four Mentalities reveal how success is often misunderstood, shaping an organization's ability—or inability—to cultivate excellence. Embracing the Mission Aligned Data Driven mentality challenges organizations to redefine success as a balance of purpose, innovation, and measurable impact.

REFLECTION

The way your organization defines and measures success can either propel it toward excellence or hold it back. Examining these mindsets can help you uncover hidden barriers and consider how new perspectives may create better alignment with your mission.

- **Assess:** *Which mentality—Compliance, Service, Results, or MADD—best describes how your organization currently measures success, and why?*

- **Reflect:** *In what ways might your current mindset prioritize compliance, activity, or misaligned results over meaningful, mission-driven impact?*

- **Act:** *What is one step your organization can take today to promote a Mission Aligned Data Driven (MADD) mentality and align your actions with your mission?*

CHAPTER 3
THE FRAMEWORK

TURNING INSIGHTS INTO ACTION

Pursuing excellence takes more than good intentions—it requires a clear, structured approach rooted in purpose, discipline, and continuous learning. As I worked with organizations across the country, I began searching for ways to help leaders think differently: to align their daily efforts with the deeper mission they served, and to move from compliance-driven habits to truly transformational practice.

Given my long-standing experience in the Community Action Network, it was natural to begin with a framework I knew well—one already designed to promote accountability and results. Grounded in rigorous research and developed by experts in the anti-poverty field, the *Community Action Accountability Framework* includes three core elements: *Results Oriented Management and Accountability (ROMA),* the *CSBG Organizational Standards,* and the *CSBG Standards of Excellence.* Together, these tools provide a practical, field-tested structure for organizational growth and impact.

Though originally created for Community Action Agencies, the values embedded in this framework—transparency, strategic alignment, and continuous improvement—are universally relevant. When approached with intention, they offer all mission-driven organizations a foundation for long-term success. More than a compliance requirement, this framework becomes a launchpad for excellence—especially when embedded into culture and aligned with purpose.

RESULTS ORIENTED MANAGEMENT AND ACCOUNTABILITY

At the heart of this framework lies *Results Oriented Management and Accountability (ROMA)*. Developed in the mid-1990s in response to the Government Performance and Results Act (GPRA) of 1993, ROMA shifted the focus from service delivery to the achievement of meaningful, measurable outcomes—a philosophy that remains vital today.

ROMA's cyclical process—*Assessment, Planning, Implementation, Results, and Evaluation*—ensures organizations remain adaptive, using their successes and challenges as opportunities to refine strategies continuously. This outcome-driven approach requires organizations to ask a vital question: *Are we making a difference?*

As a ROMA Master Trainer, I've witnessed the transformative power of this process firsthand. Organizations that embrace ROMA as a dynamic tool—not merely a compliance requirement—achieve greater alignment, efficiency, and impact. They move beyond "doing good" to delivering measurable change that reflects their mission. ROMA empowers organizations to think critically, act strategically, and adapt to evolving community needs.

CSBG ORGANIZATIONAL STANDARDS

The *Community Services Block Grant (CSBG) Organizational Standards* contribute to the framework by helping nonprofits build operational strength and accountability. First implemented in 2015, these standards set expectations in governance, leadership, planning, and financial oversight—areas that are essential for long-term organizational health.

Although developed specifically for CSBG-funded agencies, the principles they promote—strong leadership, community engagement, ethical oversight, and data-informed strategy—are important for all organizations. When approached as tools for learning and growth, the standards support both stability and innovation.

The real power of the standards emerges when they are used not just to check boxes, but to drive continuous improvement. Agencies that adopt this mindset use the standards to reflect, assess, and strengthen alignment between their mission, values, and day-to-day operations.

When leadership teams treat the standards as a foundation—not a finish line—they unlock a culture of collaboration, trust, and progress. These organizations are better positioned to weather external challenges and pursue excellence with intention.

CSBG STANDARDS OF EXCELLENCE

Building on the stability provided by the *CSBG Organizational Standards*, the *CSBG Standards of Excellence* challenge organizations to embrace industry best practices. These aspirational principles encourage organizations to think boldly, act strategically, and lead with purpose.

The *Standards of Excellence* are not about meeting minimum requirements—they inspire organizations to align their vision with action, creating meaningful and measurable change. By reflecting on their mission and evaluating whether their programs and strategies are achieving long-term impact, organizations can reimagine their potential and embrace a culture of continuous improvement.

Organizations that adopt the *Standards of Excellence* often experience a profound cultural shift. Leadership teams move from focusing on compliance to driving innovation. Staff feel empowered by a shared vision, and stakeholders are inspired by the organization's commitment to creating lasting impact.

BUILDING ON THE FOUNDATION

As I worked alongside leaders and teams striving to deliver meaningful impact, I began asking a pivotal question: *What else could we integrate to strengthen this foundation?* The goal was never to replace what worked, but to enhance it—to build on the strengths of ROMA, the CSBG Organizational Standards, and the Standards of Excellence by thoughtfully integrating methodologies that have supported high-performing businesses in other sectors.

That exploration led to the development of the Mission Aligned Data Driven approach, and ultimately, to the creation of the INSPIRE framework. Along the way, I identified six additional methodologies that could augment and support the existing Community Action foundation—not as replacements, but as practical tools to help meet today's challenges: Six Sigma, Lean, PMP, Agile/Scrum, Hoshin Kanri, and Data-Driven Decision-Making (DDDM).

THE FRAMEWORK

Although originally developed for the private sector, the principles of these methodologies transcend industry boundaries. When adapted thoughtfully, they offer nonprofits the tools to maximize efficiency, foster collaboration, and drive meaningful impact. Together, these methodologies amplify the framework's foundational elements of accountability, transparency, and continuous improvement.

Six Sigma: Reducing Variability and Driving Efficiency

Six Sigma originated in the 1980s at Motorola as a method to improve manufacturing quality and efficiency. It gained prominence in the 1990s when General Electric adopted it under the leadership of Jack Welch, showcasing its potential to transform operational performance. Six Sigma's core purpose is to reduce defects and variability in processes, ensuring consistent, high-quality products. It uses data-driven analysis and a structured methodology—DMAIC (*Define, Measure, Analyze, Improve, Control*)—to identify inefficiencies, implement solutions, and sustain improvements.[1]

At its heart, Six Sigma seeks to eliminate variability that can lead to inconsistent experiences for customers. In a manufacturing context, this might mean ensuring that every product meets a specific standard of quality. For nonprofits, the principles translate into ensuring that every client receives consistent, equitable services. Variability in service delivery can undermine trust and impact outcomes, making Six Sigma a valuable tool for organizations striving for excellence.

One powerful application of Six Sigma for nonprofits is in performance targeting. Nonprofits often set ambitious outcome goals but may experience gaps between their targets and actual results. Six Sigma introduces the concept of "defects" as deviations from these targets, helping organizations pinpoint inefficiencies in how resources are allocated or services delivered.

For instance, a workforce development nonprofit might use Six Sigma tools like root cause analysis and process mapping to identify disparities in client outcomes across locations. These insights allow the organization to standardize best practices, reducing inconsistencies and achieving a more predictable, mission-driven impact.

THE FRAMEWORK

Six Sigma's role in the broader framework is twofold: it complements ROMA's focus on mission-driven outcomes by ensuring efficiency in how those outcomes are achieved. While ROMA asks whether organizations are doing the "right things," Six Sigma asks whether they are doing those things in the "right way." This balance between effectiveness and efficiency is essential for nonprofits operating under tight budgets and high expectations.

"ROMA asks, 'Are we doing the right things?' Six Sigma asks, 'Are we doing things the right way?'"

By integrating Six Sigma into their operational framework, organizations can foster a culture of precision and measurable improvement. This methodology helps identify inefficiencies, enhance service consistency, and turn data into actionable insight—all of which strengthen an organization's ability to fulfill its mission. Ultimately, Six Sigma empowers nonprofits not only to set ambitious goals, but to achieve them with confidence, clarity, and repeatable success.

Lean: Eliminating Waste and Maximizing Value

Lean traces its roots to mid-20th century Japan, particularly through the Toyota Production System (TPS). Spearheaded by Taiichi Ohno, Lean revolutionized manufacturing by focusing on eliminating waste (*muda* in Japanese), improving efficiency, and maximizing value for the customer.[2,3] Over time, its principles have evolved beyond manufacturing and are now widely used across sectors, including healthcare, education, and nonprofits.

At its core, Lean emphasizes the relentless pursuit of value—ensuring that every action, process, and resource contributes meaningfully to the end user's needs. For nonprofits, this means maximizing the impact of services on the communities they serve. Lean's focus on identifying and eliminating waste—such as redundant processes, excess inventory, and waiting times—helps streamline operations and reduce inefficiencies.

Lean also champions *Kaizen*, or continuous improvement, which fosters a culture where employees at all levels are empowered to identify inefficiencies and propose solutions. By leveraging frontline insights, organizations build trust, promote inclusion, and drive innovation—all while improving operational effectiveness.

Tools like value stream mapping and the 5S system (*Sort, Set in Order, Shine, Standardize, Sustain*) provide nonprofits with practical methods for visualizing workflows and implementing structured improvements. These tools help ensure that every resource is used thoughtfully, every action is intentional, and every outcome aligns with the mission.

By integrating Lean principles, organizations can do more with less—not by working harder, but by working smarter. The result is a system that is impactful, sustainable, and driven by the needs of those it serves.

PMP: Structured Project Management for Complex Goals

The Project Management Professional (PMP) certification, developed by the Project Management Institute (PMI), has long been regarded as the gold standard in project management. Originally designed to standardize practices across industries, PMP offers a structured framework for planning, executing, and monitoring complex initiatives. Its processes ensure projects are delivered on time, within budget, and aligned with strategic goals.[4]

The PMP methodology is built on five process groups: *Initiating, Planning, Executing, Monitoring and Controlling, and Closing.* Although PMI's 7th edition of the PMBOK® Guide emphasizes performance domains over process groups, the traditional five-process framework remains widely used to structure and manage complex initiatives. These groups outline a sequence of activities that ensure projects are thoroughly scoped, implemented, and evaluated for lessons learned.

Supported by ten knowledge areas—covering everything from risk management and stakeholder engagement to cost control and quality assurance—PMP equips organizations to implement even the most intricate initiatives confidently.

For nonprofits, PMP adds discipline and structure to operations. For example, a nonprofit launching a workforce development program could use PMP to create a detailed project plan that aligns with funder expectations, engages community stakeholders, and ensures timely delivery of results. Projects are evaluated for alignment with the organization's mission and long-term goals, ensuring that resources are directed to initiatives with the greatest impact.

A standout feature of PMP is its emphasis on stakeholder engagement. For nonprofits, stakeholders include funders, clients, team members, legislators, and community members. PMP's tools for stakeholder analysis and communication planning ensure transparency and alignment throughout the project lifecycle, fostering trust and collaboration.

PMP also emphasizes risk management, helping organizations anticipate potential barriers and develop contingency plans to maintain progress. Its structured approach to reflection and learning ensures that every completed project contributes to continuous improvement.

By integrating PMP, nonprofits can manage complexity, maintain alignment, and deliver results that advance their mission. This approach ensures that every initiative is not only well-executed but also purpose-driven, reinforcing long-term organizational success.

Agile/Scrum: Flexibility and Iterative Development

The Agile and Scrum methodologies emerged from the software development industry's need for adaptability in rapidly changing environments. Scrum, first introduced by Ken Schwaber and Jeff Sutherland in the mid-1990s, provided a flexible project management framework based on short development cycles called sprints. In 2001, the Agile Manifesto brought together several iterative methodologies, including Scrum, and formalized a shared set of values focused on collaboration, continuous improvement, and responsiveness to change.[5,6]

For nonprofits, the adaptability of Agile/Scrum is transformative. These methodologies emphasize delivering value quickly and efficiently by breaking complex projects into manageable components. Each sprint concludes with tangible progress—such as launching a pilot program or refining service delivery processes—while retaining the flexibility to adjust strategies based on new information or stakeholder needs.

THE FRAMEWORK

A hallmark of Agile/Scrum is its focus on feedback and learning. After each sprint, teams conduct reviews and retrospectives to evaluate progress, identify areas for improvement, and make timely adjustments. For example, a nonprofit piloting a workforce development program might learn during a sprint retrospective that clients need additional digital literacy support, prompting immediate changes to better meet their needs.

Agile/Scrum also promotes collaboration through regular stand-up meetings and sprint reviews that foster open communication and shared problem-solving. For nonprofits addressing complex, interrelated issues like poverty or housing insecurity, this approach encourages alignment across departments and programs.

> "At regular intervals, the team reflects on how to become more effective, then tunes and adjusts its behavior accordingly."
>
> -Agile Principle #12

By emphasizing iteration, transparency, and responsiveness, Agile/Scrum empowers organizations to stay nimble while delivering lasting impact. Its principles create a dynamic, evolving system—one designed to meet the shifting needs of communities, one sprint at a time.

Hoshin Kanri: Aligning Strategy with Execution

Hoshin Kanri, developed in Japan during the 1960s and later adopted by companies like Toyota, is a methodology that translates high-level strategic goals into actionable plans. Often referred to as "policy deployment," it ensures alignment between an organization's long-term vision and its daily operations, connecting every action to broader goals and fostering unity and purpose across all levels.[7]

One of the most distinctive features of Hoshin Kanri is its emphasis on simplicity. By distilling complex strategies into clear, focused priorities, this methodology makes success easy to understand for leaders, staff, and stakeholders alike. Simplicity is essential not only for execution but also for engagement, ensuring everyone in the organization can see how their efforts contribute to larger goals.

Central to this approach is the "catchball" process—a collaborative dialogue between leadership and staff. Catchball ensures that strategies are not imposed from the top down but are refined through feedback at all levels of the organization. This iterative exchange fosters clarity, builds buy-in, and ensures alignment across teams. For nonprofits, where communication and engagement are critical, catchball strengthens the connection between strategy and execution, empowering staff at all levels to take ownership of their roles in achieving organizational goals.

Hoshin Kanri also prioritizes focus, encouraging organizations to concentrate their resources on a small number of initiatives with the greatest potential for transformative impact. This disciplined approach prevents overextension, reinforces simplicity, and ensures that efforts are measurable and impactful. By narrowing priorities, organizations can track progress more effectively and celebrate success along the way.

THE FRAMEWORK

A cornerstone of Hoshin Kanri is the *Plan-Do-Check-Act* (PDCA) cycle, which supports continuous improvement. This iterative process allows organizations to test strategies, evaluate outcomes, and refine actions, ensuring adaptability in dynamic environments.

By integrating Hoshin Kanri, organizations adopt a disciplined yet collaborative approach to strategic planning. Its principles turn complexity into clarity, creating a unified path to achieving meaningful and measurable outcomes. Leaders, staff, and stakeholders can align their efforts with confidence, driving results that reflect the organization's mission with purpose and simplicity.[8]

Data-Driven Decision-Making: Grounding Actions in Evidence

Data-Driven Decision-Making (DDDM) is a cornerstone of modern organizational management, emphasizing decisions informed by objective data rather than intuition or assumptions. In the nonprofit sector, where resources are limited and challenges are multifaceted, DDDM provides a framework for optimizing performance, ensuring accountability, and aligning efforts with measurable outcomes.[9,10,11]

At its core, DDDM begins with the intentional selection of meaningful metrics—those directly tied to an organization's mission and strategic goals. The focus isn't on collecting vast amounts of data but on gathering the right data—information that will actively inform decision-making. This ensures that every data point serves a purpose, guiding both internal strategies and external communications.

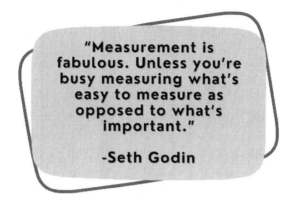

"Measurement is fabulous. Unless you're busy measuring what's easy to measure as opposed to what's important."

-Seth Godin

Once metrics are established, analysis becomes the heart of DDDM. By uncovering patterns, trends, and correlations, organizations can gain actionable insights into their operations and impact. For example, a nonprofit addressing food insecurity might analyze data to pinpoint neighborhoods with the greatest unmet needs. Advanced tools, such as predictive analytics, can also anticipate challenges or opportunities, enabling organizations to act proactively rather than reactively.

The true power of DDDM lies in its application to decision-making processes. Data isn't collected for its own sake but is intentionally used to guide resource allocation, redesign service models, and prioritize initiatives. By continuously analyzing and refining strategies based on results, nonprofits not only improve outcomes but also enhance resource utilization.[12] For example, understanding how effectively resources align with outcome targets can reveal inefficiencies and inform future planning.

Beyond operational improvements, DDDM strengthens transparency and stakeholder trust. When data is used to demonstrate outcomes to funders, clients, and the broader community, it reinforces accountability and builds confidence in the organization's

THE FRAMEWORK

mission. This transparency also fosters collaboration, aligning stakeholders around shared goals and measurable results.

By grounding actions in evidence, DDDM enables organizations to shift from anecdotal success to intentional, mission-aligned impact. Nonprofits that integrate DDDM into their operations gain a scalable approach to performance management, empowering them to adapt, optimize, and thrive regardless of size or resources. Whether through simple tracking systems or advanced analytics, the principles of DDDM ensure that every decision is purposeful, data-driven, and aligned with the organization's vision for change.[13]

Other Methodologies

Beyond the six core methodologies, a broader set of proven tools also contributes to organizational excellence. These additional approaches—while not the primary pillars of the MADD framework—offer complementary strengths that enhance adaptability, focus, and execution across diverse nonprofit settings.

Many of these tools originated in the private sector but have since been adapted to meet the unique needs of mission-driven organizations. Together, they provide a flexible and holistic toolkit for aligning strategy, performance, and impact.

- **Kanban**: A system designed to manage workflows visually, Kanban reduces inefficiencies by limiting work in progress and ensuring steady, incremental progress—perfect for nonprofits balancing multiple tasks and limited resources.[14,15,16]

- **Balanced Scorecard**: This performance management tool evaluates success through financial, customer, internal processes, and learning perspectives, providing nonprofits with a multi-faceted view of their impact and alignment with goals.[17,18]

- **Objectives and Key Results (OKR)**: By linking objectives to measurable outcomes, OKR enables nonprofits to maintain focus and accountability, driving mission-centered impact.[19,20]

- **Entrepreneurial Operating System (EOS)**: EOS aligns teams by simplifying processes, clarifying vision, and ensuring consistent execution—essential for nonprofits navigating diverse stakeholder needs.[21,22]

- **Management by Objectives (MBO)**: This system integrates individual and team goals with organizational priorities, fostering accountability and encouraging continuous improvement.[23]

- **Four Disciplines of Execution (4DX)**: With a focus on prioritizing key goals, tracking actionable measures, and maintaining accountability, 4DX empowers nonprofits to achieve measurable success in complex initiatives.[24]

- **OGSM (Objectives, Goals, Strategies, and Measures)**: OGSM translates high-level objectives into actionable plans, offering nonprofits a clear framework for strategic alignment and resource optimization.[25]

- **Three Horizons:** This model helps organizations balance present-day needs with long-term transformation by organizing strategies across three time horizons—stabilizing the current system, investing in emerging innovations, and envisioning future breakthroughs.[26]

Each methodology enhances nonprofit efficiency and impact by aligning actions with mission-driven goals. Together, they exemplify a commitment to innovation, equipping organizations to navigate challenges and sustain meaningful growth.

THE INSPIRE FRAMEWORK

What began as a mission to help leaders reconnect with their organization's purpose soon evolved into something more than a philosophy. Over time, it became a practical, adaptable framework for turning mission into measurable impact.

What sets INSPIRE apart is its ability to transform fragmented efforts into a seamless, mission-driven system. Rooted in the Mission Aligned Data Driven (MADD) mentality—a mindset that emphasizes purpose, alignment, and data-informed decisions—and informed by both the CSBG accountability framework and high-impact methodologies from other sectors, INSPIRE bridges the gap between lofty aspirations and actionable steps. It empowers leaders to align purpose with performance and accountability with measurable impact, creating a framework that is both practical and transformative.

Each of the seven elements of the *INSPIRE* framework draws on these methodologies, offering a clear roadmap for navigating the journey from defining purpose to achieving sustainable growth:

- **Identity**: Clarity of purpose is foundational to success. This step defines the mission, vision, values, beliefs, and goals that drive the organization forward, ensuring alignment with its reason for existing.

- **Navigation**: Progress begins with understanding. This step assesses the landscape to identify barriers that could hinder the ability of the organization to fulfill its purpose.

- **Strategy**: Turning vision into action requires thoughtful planning. This step ensures that goals are translated into simple, actionable, and accountable plans that align with the organization's mission and strategically eliminate identified barriers.

- **Performance**: Execution is where plans become reality. This step emphasizes implementing strategies with precision and accountability, ensuring consistency and adaptability as the organization works toward its goals.

- **Inspection**: Reflection fuels improvement. This step evaluates performance to uncover strengths, challenges, and opportunities for growth, ensuring that lessons learned lead to better outcomes.

- **Reporting**: Transparency strengthens trust. This step focuses on sharing progress and impact with stakeholders, fostering confidence and ensuring accountability to the mission.

- **Enrichment**: Growth is a continuous process. This step transforms lessons learned into actionable improvements while ensuring that successful practices are institutionalized for long-term sustainability. By continuously building capacity, refining systems, and fostering innovation, organizations create a culture of resilience and adaptability.

By simplifying complexity and uniting purpose with performance, the *INSPIRE* framework offers organizations a system of alignment and accountability that drives meaningful and measurable outcomes. Each element reinforces the next, creating a dynamic cycle of growth that supports organizations in achieving their mission while remaining adaptable to change.

Excellence is not a static destination—it is a journey shaped by intention, reflection, and the relentless pursuit of purpose. The *INSPIRE* framework empowers organizations to navigate this journey with clarity, confidence, and resilience.

FINAL THOUGHTS

At its core, the *INSPIRE* framework embodies the mentalities introduced earlier: the simplicity and clarity of Hoshin Kanri, the value alignment and waste reduction of Lean, the precision and consistency of Six Sigma, the adaptability and collaboration of Agile/Scrum, and the intentionality and focus of Data-Driven Decision-Making. These principles are not abstract concepts—they are the building blocks of transformative, measurable change.

INSPIRE challenges organizations to embrace these mentalities as part of their DNA, fostering a culture of resilience, collaboration, and continuous improvement. By aligning purpose with performance and strategy with execution, organizations can move beyond surface-level achievements to create lasting impact. It is not about doing more but doing what matters—ensuring that every action is intentional, every resource is maximized, and every outcome reflects the mission.

Excellence is not a destination; it is a commitment to progress, reflection, and purpose-driven growth. The *INSPIRE* framework provides the tools and mindset needed to turn challenges into opportunities, aspirations into actions, and visions into enduring legacies. For organizations willing to think boldly and act strategically, *INSPIRE* offers not just a roadmap but a path to sustainable excellence.

REFLECTION

As you consider how the *INSPIRE* framework could elevate your organization, reflect on the following questions to gauge your readiness and next steps:

- **Assess:** *Which tools, frameworks, or methodologies does your organization currently use to measure and improve performance? Are they effective?*

- **Reflect:** *Where do gaps exist in your current processes that hinder your organization's ability to achieve efficiency or growth?*

- **Act:** *What one step can your leadership team take to begin implementing a more structured approach, such as the INSPIRE framework, to elevate your mission?*

CHAPTER 4
GETTING STARTED

LAYING THE FOUNDATION FOR SUCCESS

Excellence doesn't begin with action—it begins with preparation. The *INSPIRE* framework provides a structured pathway to improvement, but its success depends on laying a solid foundation before the work even begins. This involves careful planning, resource alignment, and an unwavering commitment to accountability throughout the process.

The first step is to establish clear oversight, identify the necessary resources, and build a dedicated team to guide the process with focus and purpose. These foundational actions ensure that every phase of the framework is approached with clarity, collaboration—and the collective effort required for success.

Preparation isn't about checking boxes—it's about fostering a mindset of intentionality rooted in the mission. By setting the stage with thoughtful groundwork, organizations can avoid common pitfalls and approach the *INSPIRE* journey with confidence and momentum.

THE INSPIRE COMMITTEE

Implementing the *INSPIRE* framework begins with the assembly of a dedicated team to champion the process. This group plays a pivotal role in ensuring the framework's successful execution while aligning every step with the organization's mission and goals. Although the name of the committee can reflect the organization's culture, its purpose remains consistent: to inspire the organization to fulfill its purpose with excellence.

The committee's responsibilities directly align with the stages of the *INSPIRE* framework. As part of the Identity stage, the committee helps facilitate staff engagement and may recommend updates to the mission, vision, or values—or reaffirm what already exists—to the governing body, laying the groundwork for every subsequent step. In the Navigation and Strategy stages, it will ensure that plans are rooted in data-driven insights and actionable goals. Finally, throughout Inspection, Reporting, and Enrichment, the committee will monitor progress, evaluate outcomes, and foster a culture of continuous improvement.

The INSPIRE Committee is more than a task force—it's the culture shift team.

The composition of the committee is key to its effectiveness. It should include representatives from the organization's core leadership team, such as finance, human resources, public relations, IT, and program management. This diversity ensures a range of expertise and perspectives that enhance decision-making. Also, including board members will strengthen the connection between governance and implementation, ensuring alignment with the organization's strategic direction.

The *INSPIRE* Committee serves as a critical mechanism for shifting organizational mindsets. For organizations previously confined by the Compliance or Service Mentalities, the committee acts as a catalyst for change, fostering accountability, intentionality, and alignment with the mission. By bridging silos, aligning resources, and emphasizing collaboration, the committee transforms fragmented efforts into a cohesive strategy for mission-driven excellence.

BALANCING TIME, SKILLS, AND RESOURCES

Successfully implementing the *INSPIRE* framework requires intentional planning and strategic allocation of tasks, skills, and resources. Each phase of the framework introduces unique demands, and resource alignment ensures that these stages are navigated with precision and purpose.

For example, during the Navigation stage, the organization must allocate resources to gather and analyze data on community needs, internal performance, and best practices. The Strategy stage may require specialized expertise in project management or strategic planning to craft a roadmap aligned with the organization's goals. The Performance, Inspection, and Reporting phases require resources to implement, evaluate, and communicate progress to stakeholders.

The *INSPIRE* Committee plays a central role in managing this alignment. By evaluating the scope of work for each stage, the committee ensures that time, skills, and financial resources are deployed effectively. This strategic approach minimizes inefficiencies, reduces burnout, and ensures that every action advances the organization's mission.

Evaluating Team Expertise and Capacity

Once the scope of work is defined, the next step is assessing the organization's current capacity. This involves a candid evaluation of the skills, experience, and availability of team members. Many organizations find that while expertise in areas such as data analysis, project management, or compliance may already exist within the team, balancing these responsibilities with ongoing operational demands is a challenge.

The *INSPIRE* Committee must address this tension by asking key questions: *Do existing team members have the bandwidth to take on additional responsibilities without risking burnout? Are there opportunities to provide staff with training to take on new roles?* These considerations require honest discussions about workload distribution and the feasibility of reallocating duties.

Allocating Financial Resources Wisely

A realistic assessment of the organization's financial resources is critical for supporting *INSPIRE's* implementation. The committee must evaluate the budget and determine how much can be allocated toward hiring additional staff or engaging external consultants to address identified gaps.

While relying solely on internal resources may appear more economical, there are cases where external expertise offers greater value. Consultants bring specialized knowledge, helping organizations avoid pitfalls and accelerate progress. Additionally, because many tasks in the *INSPIRE* framework occur cyclically, hiring full-time staff for intermittent responsibilities may not be cost-effective. Bundled pricing or annual retainer agreements with consultants can offer cost-effective solutions that fit within tight budgets.

Balancing Internal and External Support

Ultimately, whether tasks are handled internally, outsourced, or approached through a hybrid model depends on the organization's unique needs and capacity. The *INSPIRE* Committee plays a pivotal role in guiding these decisions, ensuring resources—whether time, talent, or financial—are deployed strategically to maximize efficiency and impact.

By aligning tasks, skills, and resources, organizations can confidently move forward, knowing their efforts are rooted in a thoughtful and sustainable plan. This intentionality creates the foundation for success while fostering a culture of accountability and collaboration throughout the framework's implementation.

FINAL THOUGHTS

Beginning the journey with the *INSPIRE* framework is about preparation, alignment, and intentionality. Establishing the *INSPIRE* Committee, identifying key resources, and thoughtfully balancing internal capacity with external expertise set the stage for success. These foundational steps ensure your organization is equipped to navigate the framework with focus and purpose.

Preparation is not just a logistical exercise—it is the cornerstone of achieving excellence. As explored in Chapters 1 and 2, true excellence requires clarity of purpose, intentionality, and bold leadership. By prioritizing collaboration, accountability, and strategic resource allocation at this stage, you create a culture that supports sustainable progress and mission-driven impact.

As we transition to the next chapter, we'll explore the first step of the *INSPIRE* framework: Identity. Defining who you are, the values you stand for, and the problem you seek to solve will serve as the cornerstone of your organization's transformation. With the foundation firmly in place, the work of building a legacy of excellence begins.

REFLECTION

Use the following questions to guide your preparation for the journey ahead:

- **Assess:** *Does your organization have the right people, resources, and structures in place to implement the INSPIRE framework effectively?*

- **Reflect:** *What internal gaps or challenges might limit your ability to pursue excellence through this framework?*

- **Act:** *What one step can your leadership team take today to build readiness for implementation?*

CHAPTER 5
IDENTITY

A STRONG FOUNDATION

When I was a child, one of my favorite Sunday School songs was about the wise man who built his house on the rock and the foolish man who built his house on the sand. I can still remember the hand motions we used as we sang about the rains coming down, the floods coming up, and the house on the sand falling flat. Even then, the lesson was clear: a strong foundation is critical. The wise man's house stood firm because it was built on something solid, while the foolish man's house collapsed because it lacked that stability.

Although the song refers to Jesus as the ultimate foundation, the principle applies universally. Every organization needs a strong foundation so they can weather life's storms. Identity is that foundation. It's the bedrock upon which everything else is built. Just as a sturdy house needs a firm base to endure rain, wind, and floods, an organization must be grounded in its purpose. Without this clarity, an organization is like the house on the sand, vulnerable to shifting priorities, external pressures, or internal misalignment.

A strong identity is more than just knowing your mission statement—it's about answering the critical questions that define your value and guide every decision: *Why do we exist? What is the problem we are addressing? How will the community be better because of our work?* These are not abstract musings; they are the foundation for everything an organization does, from day-to-day operations to long-term strategies.

Identity is the foundation. Everything else is built on it.

Organizations with a firm foundation of identity stand out because they know who they are and what they're working toward. They can weather funding shifts, respond to evolving community needs, and adapt to unexpected challenges without losing focus. Identity keeps them grounded, aligned, and purposeful, ensuring that their actions always lead back to their mission.

The house built on the rock didn't just survive—it thrived. Its foundation gave it strength to endure and succeed, even when the storms came. Identity does the same for organizations. It ensures that their efforts are built to last, aligning purpose with action and providing a clear, unshakable foundation for everything they do.

LISTENING TO THE VOICES OF THE TEAM

Great leaders know that strong organizational identities are built collaboratively. The people who bring your mission to life—your board, staff, and volunteers—hold unique perspectives that provide invaluable insights into your purpose and values. Listening to their voices not only deepens understanding but fosters a culture of trust and shared ownership over the organization's direction.

This input can be gathered through a variety of methods, including:

- **Surveys:** Efficiently collect feedback from a broad cross-section of the team, particularly those who may not have time for in-depth discussions. Surveys can explore questions such as, *"What do you see as the core purpose of our organization?"* or *"What values best describe how we operate?"*

- **Focus Groups:** These small, facilitated discussions uncover deeper themes, allowing participants to explore the organization's mission and values collectively.

- **Interviews:** Conversations provide additional context and depth, capturing perspectives shaped by the subject's unique roles and experiences.

The key to success in this step is creating a process that allows every voice to be heard. While the *INSPIRE* Committee and governing body will ultimately refine and finalize the organization's mission, vision, values, and goals, involving the broader team ensures inclusivity and builds trust. When staff and volunteers see their input reflected in the organization's identity, they develop a deeper connection to its purpose. This alignment fosters a culture of collaboration and commitment, creating momentum for the work ahead.

This inclusive approach also has practical benefits. Staff and volunteers often have firsthand knowledge of the challenges faced by the community and the impact of the organization's programs, offering invaluable insights into the problem the organization exists to address. Board members bring a strategic and governance-oriented perspective that ensures the identity aligns with the organization's long-term goals. Together, these voices provide a comprehensive view that enriches the process and ensures the resulting identity reflects the full scope of the organization's work and culture.

By intentionally involving the entire organization in this process, the INSPIRE Committee lays the groundwork for a strong, cohesive identity and sets the tone for a culture of engagement and accountability. These early steps create a foundation that will carry the organization through the rest of the INSPIRE process, ensuring alignment with its purpose and building the trust and commitment needed to achieve excellence.

DEFINING THE PROBLEM

The first question that must be answered is what problem the organization exists to solve. Every nonprofit is born out of a desire to address a specific need or challenge within its community. Defining that problem with clarity and precision is the first step in building an authentic and mission-driven identity.

For many organizations, this process involves challenging assumptions. The *INSPIRE* Committee may start by identifying what they believe the problem to be and how it impacts the local community, but assumptions alone are not enough. Data is essen-

IDENTITY

tial for verifying and refining these beliefs. By presenting quantitative and qualitative information, organizations can ground their understanding of the problem in reality and ensure a shared foundation for decision-making.

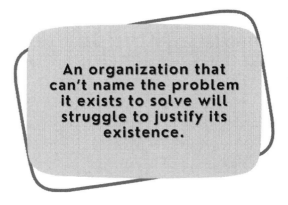

An organization that can't name the problem it exists to solve will struggle to justify its existence.

While every organization's focus may differ, the challenge of poverty is a common thread for many. For the purposes of illustrating the *INSPIRE* process in this book, we will use poverty as our example.

Poverty can be broadly defined as the inability to secure the basic needs required for survival and well-being. According to *Britannica*, it is the state in which individuals lack access to essential necessities—such as food, housing, and healthcare—needed to live a life of dignity. These unmet needs form the foundation of individual and community stability and are often deeply interconnected.[1]

To better understand basic human needs, it helps to turn to the work of Abraham Maslow, a renowned psychologist best known for developing the Hierarchy of Needs. In his groundbreaking 1943 paper, *A Theory of Human Motivation,* Maslow proposed that human needs are arranged in a hierarchy, beginning with the most basic physiological and safety needs. [2]

These foundational needs must be met before individuals can pursue higher-level needs such as relationships, self-esteem, and personal growth.

Maslow's work is widely respected across disciplines because it explains how unmet basic needs create barriers to an individual's ability to thrive. In the context of poverty, his hierarchy provides a powerful framework for understanding how the inability to secure basic necessities prevents individuals and families from achieving stability, let alone flourishing. Addressing these needs is not just a matter of survival but a prerequisite for unlocking human potential.

Maslow's hierarchy of needs

The bottom two tiers of Maslow's hierarchy—physiological needs and safety needs—are the most relevant when discussing poverty. These needs represent the essentials for life and well-being. Without them, individuals are trapped in a cycle of crisis, unable to focus on anything beyond immediate survival. Let's examine these needs in the context of poverty:

- **Housing**: Housing is more than just shelter; it is the foundation of stability. Safe housing provides not only protection from the elements but also a secure environment where individuals can rest, recover, and plan for the future. A home with functioning utilities allows families to stay warm in the winter, cool in the summer, and maintain hygiene. It's a place where food can be stored and prepared, where children can study, and where adults can recharge. Without secure housing, everything else becomes harder—education, employment, and even health outcomes suffer.

- **Nutrition**: Proper nutrition is essential for physical and mental health. Access to food and water isn't enough; the food must provide the nutrients needed for bodies to grow, heal, and function optimally. Malnutrition, even in its mildest forms, can lead to long-term developmental issues in children, reduced productivity in adults, and increased vulnerability to illness. Clean water is equally critical, not only for drinking but also for cooking, cleaning, and maintaining hygiene. Nutrition is a cornerstone of well-being, and its absence perpetuates the cycle of poverty.

- **Clothing**: Clothing is often overlooked when discussing basic needs, but it plays a critical role in ensuring safety, dignity, and access to opportunities. Adequate clothing includes innerwear, outerwear, and footwear appropriate for the climate and circumstances. For example, warm clothing during winter months can prevent illnesses, while proper footwear allows individuals to travel safely to school or work. Beyond its functional purpose, clothing also fosters a sense of dignity and self-respect, which are vital for emotional well-being.

- **Wellness**: Wellness encompasses physical, emotional, and mental health, as well as safety from harm. Access to healthcare is essential for addressing both immediate needs and chronic conditions. Without these elements, individuals cannot achieve stability or focus on long-term goals.

Poverty manifests in different ways, but it can often be categorized into two levels: *Crisis Poverty* and *Vulnerable Poverty*. Understanding these distinctions helps organizations prioritize interventions and craft strategies that address both immediate and long-term needs.

- **Crisis Poverty:** Crisis poverty occurs when individuals lack access to one or more basic needs. Families experiencing homelessness, children going to bed hungry, or individuals without proper clothing during the winter are all in crisis. In these situations, the absence of basic needs creates a state of emergency where survival takes precedence over everything else. Crisis poverty demands immediate intervention to stabilize individuals and prevent further harm.

- **Vulnerable Poverty:** Vulnerable poverty describes individuals or families whose basic needs are currently met but remain precarious. For example, a family might have housing but be one paycheck away from eviction or have food today but lack consistent access to nutritious meals. Vulnerability represents a fragile stability that can be easily disrupted by external factors, such as job loss, illness, or rising costs of living. Addressing vulnerable poverty requires proactive measures to build resilience and prevent backsliding into crisis.

A VISION FOR THE FUTURE

The next step in establishing identity is translating the problem into a compelling vision statement. A vision statement serves as a North Star, articulating the organization's aspirations for the community it serves. Unlike traditional models, which often describe the long-term future of the organization itself, the *INSPIRE* framework challenges leaders to envision the future of the community once the problem has been resolved. This shift in perspective allows organizations to focus on the impact of their work rather than their internal goals. The vision becomes a true representation of success—not for the organization alone, but for the people and communities it exists to serve.

To develop a vision aligned with this approach, we recommend starting with the conditions of the problem (poverty, in this example) and imagining how these conditions would change if the organization's work were successful. What would an ideal community look like? What would life be like for the residents in that community? These questions anchor the vision statement in tangible outcomes, giving it clarity and purpose.

For example, if the problem is poverty, the organization might define the ideal conditions as a community where:

- Every family has safe, stable housing with access to utilities.

- Residents have consistent access to nutritious food and clean water.

- Individuals have access to adequate clothing, healthcare, and wellness support.

- Families are protected from the vulnerabilities of crisis and equipped with the resources to thrive.

Visioning begins by drawing on input gathered during earlier team engagement efforts. Their lived experience and direct connection to the community offer insight into what success should truly look like. These perspectives help ensure the vision reflects both organizational aspirations and real community needs.

Once the ideal conditions are identified, the next step is distilling them into a concise, inspiring statement. A great vision statement is:

1. **Short and Sharply Focused**: Avoid lengthy descriptions. The statement should be memorable and easy to communicate.

2. **Outcome-Oriented**: Focus on what success looks like for the community, not just for the organization.

3. **Bold and Aspirational**: Inspire action and confidence by painting a picture of a transformed community.

For example:

- *"A hunger-free community where every family has the resources to thrive."*

- *"A future where every child has access to safe housing, quality education, and opportunity."*

- *"A world where poverty is eliminated, and every individual lives with dignity and security."*

These statements are more than just words—they embody the organization's purpose and provide a sense of direction for everyone involved. They also create a rallying point for external stakeholders, including funders and partners, who want to understand the organization's broader vision.

Creating a vision statement is a collaborative effort, but it also requires decisive leadership. Feedback from team members, community data, and committee discussions can reveal common themes and priorities. Using tools like text analysis or categorization exercises can help identify recurring ideas or values. However, the *INSPIRE* Committee must ultimately synthesize this input into a clear and actionable statement.

In some cases, the organization may already have a vision statement that aligns with its aspirations. If so, this step might involve reaffirming that statement and ensuring it resonates with current community needs. In other cases, it may mean refining or entirely reimagining the vision to reflect a deeper understanding of the problem and its potential solutions. The key is ensuring that the final statement reflects the community's aspirations, not just the organization's ambitions.

This approach to visioning shifts the focus outward, aligning the organization's purpose with the needs and hopes of the community. By starting with the conditions of the problem and imagining how they would change, organizations craft vision statements that are not only inspiring but also grounded in measurable impact. These statements become touchstones for the organization's work, reminding everyone involved—leaders, staff, volunteers, and stakeholders—of the ultimate goal.

A strong vision inspires action. It motivates teams to align their efforts, galvanizes support from external stakeholders, and provides clarity when making decisions. With this vision in place, the organization is ready to move forward, turning aspirations into strategies and strategies into measurable outcomes.

THE MISSION: DEFINING THE PURPOSE

While the vision provides the destination, the mission describes the path. It is the declaration of the organization's purpose—its reason for being—and serves as the foundation for all decisions, actions, and strategies. As Peter Drucker famously said, "Each social sector organization exists to make a distinctive difference in the lives of individuals and in society. Making this difference is the mission—the organization's purpose and very reason for being." A strong mission captures this purpose, communicating both the value the organization brings and the impact it aims to create.

The mission statement is more than a tagline or a public relations tool. It is the embodiment of the organization's purpose, which is

IDENTITY

what gives it value. Drawing on principles from methodologies like Hoshin Kanri and Lean, the mission focuses the organization's efforts on what truly matters: creating value for its community and stakeholders. By articulating the purpose clearly and concisely, the mission ensures that every program, service, and strategy aligns with this core value proposition.

In Lean philosophy, anything that does not deliver value is considered waste. Similarly, Hoshin Kanri emphasizes aligning actions and resources with the organization's highest priorities. A clear mission statement acts as a compass, guiding resource allocation and decision-making to eliminate inefficiencies and drive impactful outcomes.

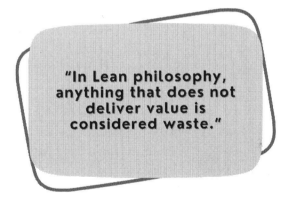

"In Lean philosophy, anything that does not deliver value is considered waste."

According to ROMA principles, an effective mission statement addresses four essential elements that clarify the organization's role and purpose:

- **Population**: The mission must specify the primary population or community the organization serves. This clarity ensures that all stakeholders understand who the organization is designed to help. *Example: "Low-income families in rural communities."*

- **Outcome**: The mission should outline the desired change or impact the organization strives to achieve for its population. This reinforces the organization's commitment to measurable results. *Example: "Achieving long-term self-sufficiency and stability."*

- **Strategy**: The mission must describe, in broad terms, how the organization will address the problem or achieve its outcomes. This provides a roadmap for program design and service delivery. *Example: "Through education, advocacy, and community partnerships."*

- **Relationship**: Acknowledge the collaborative nature of nonprofit work by referencing partnerships and external relationships that support the mission. *Example: "Working with local businesses, schools, and healthcare providers."*

By addressing these four components, the mission statement bridges the gap between the problem the organization seeks to solve and the vision for the future.

Creating a mission statement begins with strategic refinement. Earlier insights from staff, board members, and internal stakeholders have already helped clarify the organization's priorities. The INSPIRE Committee's task is now to distill that collective understanding into a concise, impactful statement that captures the organization's core purpose and aspirations.

While input is critical, clarity is paramount. The mission statement should be:

- **Short and sharply focused**: Avoid jargon and lengthy descriptions. A mission statement should be memorable and easy to communicate.

- **Broad but specific**: It must encompass all the organization's work while remaining focused on its core purpose.

- **Grounded in purpose**: The mission is not about organizational survival or internal operations; it's about the difference the organization seeks to make.

An effective mission statement is more than words on paper—it's a tool for alignment. It informs strategic planning, guides program development, and provides a basis for evaluating success. When an organization's actions align with its mission, it creates a cohesive, focused environment where every effort contributes to the same overarching purpose.

The attached checklist serves as a guide for evaluating and refining mission statements. Key questions include:

- *Does the mission clearly define the target population?*

- *Does it explain your product (outcome)?*

- *Does it explain the process (strategy) that will be used to produce the product?*

- *Does it reference the partners (relationships) that will help to produce the product?*

- *Is it inspirational, memorable, and easy to communicate?*

When crafting a mission statement for anti-poverty organizations, it's important to recognize that there are common themes that reflect the varying levels of progress organizations aim to achieve for their clients. These themes align with the levels of poverty discussed earlier—crisis and vulnerability—and expand into the realms of stability and self-sufficiency. A well-crafted mission statement should reflect the organization's role in addressing these levels and its aspirations for creating lasting impact.

Stability:

Stability represents the point at which customers have adequate resources to meet their basic needs on an ongoing basis but may rely on external subsidies. Organizations that focus on stability aim to move clients out of crisis and vulnerability by addressing immediate needs and creating a foundation for long-term improvement.

For example, an organization providing housing assistance might describe its mission as:

"To provide low-income families in our community with financial resources promoting the establishment of safe, stable housing."

While this is a critical step, stabilization alone does not always equip individuals or families for long-term independence. It is an essential milestone, particularly for vulnerable populations such as seniors or individuals with disabilities, for whom further

IDENTITY

advancement may not be feasible. However, for many, the ultimate goal is to transition beyond stability into self-sufficiency.

Self-Sufficiency:

Self-sufficiency reflects the ability of individuals or families to meet their basic needs independently, without relying on external subsidies. Within self-sufficiency, there are two degrees:

- **Safety**: Customers have adequate resources to meet their basic needs on an ongoing basis without external subsidies. This degree focuses on achieving independence in essential areas such as housing, food security, and financial stability.

- **Thriving**: Customers not only meet their basic needs independently but also have additional resources to improve their quality of life and prepare for unexpected expenses. Thriving represents the ultimate goal—where individuals can save, invest, and build a sustainable future for themselves and their families.

Organizations that provide emergency services, such as shelters or food pantries, play a vital role in helping individuals avoid crisis. However, these services often address immediate needs without significantly moving clients toward stability or self-sufficiency.

While emergency services are essential for preventing further harm, they often leave clients in a state of vulnerability, unable to achieve long-term stability without additional interventions.

For organizations with missions centered on stabilization or self-sufficiency, emergency services can act as an entry point—meeting urgent needs while creating pathways for ongoing support. For example, a homeless shelter might partner with housing agencies to transition clients into stable, long-term housing.

Even stabilization requires a long-term approach, addressing systemic barriers such as access to affordable housing, quality healthcare, or education. This is particularly true for populations such as seniors or individuals with disabilities, for whom stabilization may represent the highest achievable outcome. For others, however, the goal should be to move as many as possible into the self-sufficiency spectrum—helping them not only to survive but to thrive.

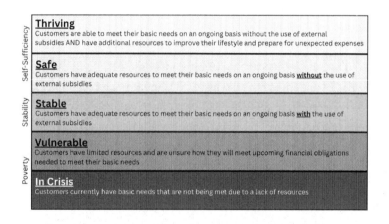

A Sample Economic Security Scale

Anti-poverty work is as much about meeting immediate needs as it is about creating pathways for independence. Whether the goal is stabilization or self-sufficiency, organizations must recognize where they fit within this continuum and craft mission statements that reflect their unique contributions to the fight against poverty.

IDENTITY

VALUES AND BELIEFS: THE HEART OF THE ORGANIZATION

An organization's values and beliefs are the cornerstone of its culture. Together, they define who the organization is, what it stands for, and how it approaches its work. While the mission describes the purpose, and the vision outlines the future, values and beliefs guide the behaviors, decisions, and interactions that shape the organization's identity—both internally and externally.

Values are the organization's core principles, expressed in single, memorable words. Words which encapsulate the essence of the organization's culture, defining how it operates and what it prioritizes. Examples might include integrity, equity, collaboration, or innovation. By focusing on single words, values remain simple, impactful, and easy to remember, ensuring they can be consistently referenced and applied in day-to-day operations.

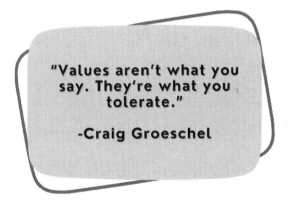

"Values aren't what you say. They're what you tolerate."

-Craig Groeschel

Keeping the list of values limited to the top three to five is critical. Overloading with too many values dilutes their power and makes them harder to implement effectively. A concise list ensures clarity, focus, and alignment, allowing the organization to channel its efforts into living out those values in everything it does.

While values capture what the organization stands for, beliefs explain why those values matter. Beliefs are the guiding statements that support or form the organization's culture. They give depth and meaning to the values, providing context for how they should be interpreted and applied.

Example:

- **Value**: Collaboration

- **Belief**: *We believe that working together strengthens communities, breaks down barriers, and creates sustainable solutions.*

These belief statements make the values actionable and relatable, connecting them to the organization's mission and vision.

As established earlier, engaging your team is essential to building a strong identity. When it comes to values and beliefs, their insight can illuminate what truly defines your organizational culture. To gather this input, consider asking questions such as:

- *What words best represent who we are as an organization?*

- *What behaviors and attitudes do we most value in our work?*

- *What do you believe sets us apart from other organizations?*

By engaging the team in this process, the organization not only ensures inclusivity but also fosters buy-in. When team members see their input reflected in the organization's values and beliefs, they develop a stronger connection to its culture and purpose.

Values and beliefs serve critical roles for both internal and external purposes:

Internally:

- **Shaping Organizational Culture**: Values and beliefs create a shared understanding of what behaviors and attitudes are expected within the organization. They guide interactions, decision-making, and problem-solving, fostering a cohesive and aligned team.

- **Building Unity**: When team members rally around shared values, it strengthens their connection to the organization's mission and vision, creating a sense of purpose and belonging.

- **Providing Guidance**: In moments of uncertainty or conflict, values act as a compass, helping the organization make decisions that align with its culture and purpose.

Externally:

- **Communicating Identity**: Values and beliefs provide stakeholders—funders, partners, and the community—with a clear sense of who the organization is and what it stands for.

- **Inspiring Trust**: By consistently living out its values, the organization builds credibility and trust with external audiences.

- **Differentiating the Organization**: Values and beliefs set the organization apart, highlighting what makes it unique in its approach and impact.

Values and beliefs complement the mission and vision by providing the cultural framework necessary to achieve them. While the mission defines the purpose and the vision describes the destination, values and beliefs shape the path forward. For example:

If the mission is to promote self-sufficiency, values like empowerment and innovation might guide how the organization approaches its programs.

If the vision is a community free from hunger, beliefs like *"We believe every individual has a right to dignity and nourishment"* reinforce the organization's commitment to that goal.

When the mission, vision, values, and beliefs are in alignment, they create a cohesive and powerful identity that drives both internal actions and external engagement.

Values and beliefs are the heartbeat of the organization. By defining them clearly and aligning them with the mission and vision, the organization creates a culture that inspires action, builds trust, and drives meaningful impact. Limiting the values to a focused set ensures clarity and consistency, while belief statements provide depth and guidance. Together, these elements empower the organization to live out its purpose and fulfill its aspirations, both within the team and in the communities it serves.

GOALS: EXPANDING THE MISSION

Organizational goals are a critical component of the *INSPIRE* framework, acting as a bridge between the organization's mission and the strategies that will bring it to life. These goals categorize the organization's work into three distinct levels:

Improving the Lives of People
Family Level

Transforming Community Infrastructure
Community Level

Building Organizational Capacity
Agency Level

While the *INSPIRE* model emphasizes the importance of SMART (Specific, Measurable, Achievable, Relevant, Time-bound) elements, those accountability details will be addressed at a lower level. At this stage, the focus is on defining clear and aspirational goals that set the direction for the organization's work and align with its mission and vision.

Organizational goals provide a framework for aligning efforts across all levels of the organization. They clarify the impact the organization seeks to achieve and offer a way to organize strategies into actionable categories. These goals help ensure that every program, initiative, and resource allocation aligns with the mission and advances the organization's broader purpose.

By categorizing goals into family, community, and agency levels, a practice adopted from the ROMA framework, the *INSPIRE* model ensures that the organization's efforts are comprehensive, balanced, and impactful.

For independent organizations, these goals are typically developed at a local level, tailored to address the unique needs and priorities of their specific communities. For Community Action Agencies (CAAs) and similar organizations, however, these goals often align with or reflect national standards or network-wide goals. This alignment ensures consistency across the field while still allowing flexibility to adapt to local needs. By aligning with broader standards, organizations reinforce their relevance within their sector while meeting the expectations of funders and stakeholders.

1. Family Level Goals

These goals focus on the individuals and families the organization serves. They are rooted in the mission's commitment to direct impact and reflect the organization's aspirations for meaningful change in the lives of those it serves.

Examples:

- *"Individuals and families with low incomes are stable and achieve economic security."* (National Community Action Goal)

- *"Individuals achieve and maintain improved health and well-being through access to comprehensive healthcare and informed decision-making."*

These goals highlight the organization's role in addressing barriers and supporting personal and family-level success.

2. Community Level Goals

Community-level goals address systemic challenges and environmental factors, focusing on creating conditions that enable individuals and families to thrive. These goals emphasize collaboration, advocacy, and systemic change.

Example:

- *"Communities where people with low incomes live are healthy and offer economic opportunity."* (National Community Action Goal)

By focusing on the broader community, these goals reflect the organization's commitment to addressing root causes and building a supportive infrastructure.

3. Goals for Building Organizational Capacity

To effectively serve individuals and communities, the organization must ensure its own strength, sustainability, and accountability. These goals focus on internal capacity-building, such as enhancing systems, processes, and resources.

Examples:

- *"The organization ensures financial stability and accountability while delivering compassionate, efficient care that aligns with its mission and values."*

- *"The organization is compliant and has established an accountability framework to deliver quality services promoting self-determination with a high level of efficiency and effectiveness."*

These goals highlight the organization's commitment to continuous improvement and operational excellence, ensuring it has the capacity to achieve its mission.

As with other elements of the *INSPIRE* framework, defining organizational goals should involve input from staff, board members, and volunteers. Engaging the team ensures that the goals reflect a shared understanding of the organization's mission and priorities while fostering buy-in and accountability.

Steps for Development:

- **Mission Alignment**: Revisit the mission to ensure that all goals directly support the organization's purpose.

- **Team Engagement**: Use surveys, brainstorming sessions, and/or focus groups to gather input on priorities and opportunities.

- **Prioritization**: Identify the top three to five goals that reflect the organization's highest priorities across the categories of family, community, and agency.

- **Refinement**: Synthesize feedback into clear, concise goals that provide direction while leaving room for flexibility in implementation.

Organizational goals expand on the mission by breaking it into actionable categories that focus on improving lives, transforming communities, and building capacity. By aligning with national standards, engaging the team, and focusing on clear priorities, these goals provide the framework for advancing the organization's mission and vision.

FINAL THOUGHTS

Identity is the cornerstone of every organization. It provides clarity about who you are, the problem you aim to solve, and the vision that drives your work forward. As the first step in the *INSPIRE* framework, Identity lays the foundation for everything that follows. Without it, the remaining stages—Navigation, Strategy, and beyond—lack the alignment and focus necessary for success.

A well-defined identity is not just a formality; it is a commitment to excellence. It ensures that every action, decision, and strategy stems from a clear purpose and reflects the organization's values. As explored in earlier chapters, achieving mission-driven excellence requires intentionality, bold leadership, and alignment at every level. Identity makes this possible by anchoring your efforts to a stable foundation.

As you prepare to move into the next step of the process, remember that a strong identity is more than words on paper—it is a guidepost for every phase of your work. With clarity about your mission, vision, values, and goals, you are now equipped to assess your environment and begin charting a path forward.

In the next chapter, we'll explore Navigation, the second step in the *INSPIRE* framework. This phase will guide you in identifying barriers, opportunities, and resources, ensuring that your strategies are grounded in both data and a clear understanding of your landscape. With your identity firmly in place, you are ready to move forward with purpose and confidence.

REFLECTION

Use the following questions to reflect on your organization's identity and its alignment with your purpose:

- **Assess:** *How clearly has your organization defined its identity through its mission, vision, values, and understanding of the core problem?*

- **Reflect:** *In what ways do these identity elements inspire your team—and where might misalignment or confusion still exist?*

- **Act:** *What one step can you take today to strengthen and clarify your organization's identity moving forward?*

CHAPTER 6
NAVIGATION

UNDERSTANDING THE LANDSCAPE

The Navigation phase is where organizations step back to evaluate the full landscape—identifying the barriers that may stand between their current situation and fulfillment of their purpose.

Navigation is not about solving problems—that comes later. It's about discovery, gaining clarity, and identifying which barriers must be addressed first. By illuminating where barriers exist—and how they impact efforts—organizations lay the groundwork for strategic, focused action in the next phase.

Barriers can exist in the lives of individuals (family level), within the broader infrastructure of the community (community level), as well as inside the organization itself (agency level). These barriers can be classified into two distinct groups:

External Barriers

External barriers are challenges that exist outside of the organization and limit its ability to fulfill its purpose. These barriers can be further separated into two sub-categories:

- **Personal Barriers:** These are obstacles that individuals or families face in their day-to-day lives, directly affecting their ability to overcome challenges. For example, unemployment may prevent someone from earning the income necessary to escape poverty, a lack of education may limit access to higher-paying jobs, and chronic health conditions may produce additional costs while restricting employment opportunities. For an organization whose goal is to fight poverty, these barriers can stand in the way of success.

- **Infrastructural Barriers**: These challenges exist within the systems and resources of the community. Unlike personal barriers, infrastructural barriers cannot be solved by working with individuals alone but require improvements to the community environment. Examples include a lack of safe and affordable housing, insufficient childcare slots, limited transportation options, food deserts, or a shortage of healthcare providers. These systemic gaps create structural limitations that restrict individuals and families from achieving stability or success.

Internal Barriers

Internal barriers are operational challenges that exist within the organization itself and can undermine its ability to respond effectively to external challenges. Examples include outdated processes, inefficient systems, staff resource gaps, or misaligned priorities. For instance, an organization with redundant intake processes may struggle to serve clients efficiently, wasting time and resources that could otherwise be used to deliver impact. By addressing internal barriers, organizations ensure they have the capacity, systems, and agility needed to fulfill their mission effectively.

Integrating Insights

By identifying and prioritizing both external and internal barriers, leaders gain a comprehensive understanding of the landscape they must navigate. Recognizing the interconnected nature of these barriers allows organizations to develop strategies that are both targeted and actionable. Personal barriers highlight the need for tailored, direct support for individuals, while infrastructural barriers point to larger systemic challenges that require long-term community-level solutions. At the same time, addressing internal barriers ensures that the organization is equipped to operate effectively, making the most of its resources and maximizing its impact.

DATA: THE FOUNDATION FOR IDENTIFYING BARRIERS

At the heart of the Navigation phase lies data—a key element of the Mission Aligned Data Driven mentality. Data transforms decision-making by grounding it in facts rather than assumptions, enabling organizations to identify the barriers that stand in the way of achieving their mission. By embracing data-driven approaches, organizations ensure clarity, precision, and alignment with their purpose as they work to overcome challenges and achieve excellence.

Data is simply the metrics that are collected, measured, and analyzed to gain insights into a problem, trend, or opportunity. It helps organizations answer key questions: *What barriers exist? How significant are they? Who is impacted? And why do these barriers persist?* Without reliable, high-quality data, organizations risk drawing inaccurate conclusions and making decisions that are disconnected from reality. Strong data ensures that strategies are focused, actionable, and mission aligned.

> "Data is simply the metrics that are collected, measured, and analyzed to gain insights into a problem, trend, or opportunity."

There are two essential types of data: quantitative and qualitative. Together, they offer a balanced, comprehensive understanding of barriers—combining measurable evidence with the experiences of those impacted.

Quantitative Data

Quantitative data is numerical information that helps organizations measure the scale and frequency of the challenges they aim to address. It answers critical questions like: *How many people are impacted? How often does this occur? What is the measurable change over time?* Because it is rooted in numbers, quantitative data provides objective evidence for identifying patterns, monitoring progress, and setting priorities.

To make the most of quantitative data, it's important to understand its various forms. Each type of quantitative data serves a unique purpose in helping organizations make informed, mission-aligned decisions.

- **Discrete Data: Counting with Whole Numbers**
  Discrete data refers to values that can be counted as whole, indivisible units. These numbers represent things that can only occur in set amounts—such as the number of children in a household or the number of households served in a year. You can't have 3.7 people in a family; the value must be whole. Discrete data helps organizations track counts and totals in a clear, definitive way. For example, the total number of people who receive utility assistance or secure employment.

- **Continuous Data: Measuring on a Spectrum**
  Continuous data captures values that can fall anywhere within a given range—even between whole numbers. It reflects measurements that can be infinitely refined. For

example, a person's income, the square footage of a home, or the number of hours worked per week are all continuous data points. These measurements can take on any value within a range, allowing for precise analysis of trends over time or across populations. Examples could include a customer's monthly income or commute times to work.

- **Interval Data: Measuring with a Scale** Interval data includes numerical values where the difference between numbers is consistent and meaningful, but the scale lacks a true zero point. This means that while you can measure how much one value differs from another, you cannot say that one value is twice as much as another. For example, the difference between 70°F and 80°F is the same as between 80°F and 90°F, but 0°F does not mean "no temperature."

- **Ratio Data: Measuring with a True Zero** Ratio data is the most precise form of quantitative data. Like interval data, it features consistent spacing between values—but with a critical distinction: it includes a true zero point. This allows for all types of mathematical operations, including multiplication and division. Because zero truly represents the absence of a value, it is possible to say that one measure is "twice as much" as another. For example, if someone has $0 in income, that indicates the complete absence of income, and their earnings can be meaningfully compared to someone making $20,000 or $40,000 annually.

Quantitative data comes from a range of trusted sources, including:

- **Government Reports:** U.S. Census Bureau, Bureau of Labor Statistics, state and local agencies.

- **Organizational Data:** Internal databases tracking customer demographics, services, and outcomes.

- **Research and Surveys:** Published studies, economic reports, or standardized community surveys.

For example, five years of economic data might reveal that unemployment rates in a particular zip code remain 20% higher than regional averages, signaling a persistent employment barrier. Similarly, an analysis of customer data might show that 60% of families accessing housing support also reported barriers related to childcare—suggesting interconnected challenges.

The strength of quantitative data lies in its ability to measure problems objectively over time, providing the evidence organizations need to prioritize action. To ensure accuracy, organizations must rely on data that is recent, multi-sourced, and reflective of long-term trends.

Qualitative Data

Qualitative data offers insight into the human side of the challenges organizations aim to address. While quantitative data answers "how much" or "how often," qualitative data explores the "how" and "why." It captures stories, perceptions, experiences, and observations, helping organizations understand the deeper context behind the numbers.

Qualitative data brings clarity to complex issues, revealing how barriers are experienced in real life and why they persist. This kind of information often comes directly from stakeholders—clients, staff, volunteers, or community members—and helps shape strategies that are both compassionate and grounded in lived reality.

- **Narrative Data: Stories that Illuminate** Narrative data refers to descriptive accounts that illustrate personal experiences and perceptions. These stories often emerge in interviews, open-ended survey responses, focus groups, or client testimonials. Narrative data helps organizations connect emotionally and intellectually with the issues they seek to solve. For example, a single parent might describe having to turn down a promotion due to a lack of reliable childcare, highlighting how a personal barrier intersects with systemic gaps.

- **Observational Data: Direct Engagement Insights** Observational data comes from witnessing behaviors, conditions, or environments firsthand. Staff, volunteers, or evaluators document what they see, offering grounded insights into how services are delivered or how systems function. These observations reveal opportunities for improvement or confirm existing patterns. For example, a case manager might note that many clients appear frustrated during the intake process, suggesting a need to streamline procedures.

- **Perceptual Data: Attitudes, Beliefs, and Feedback** Perceptual data reflects how people feel about an issue—their beliefs, opinions, or levels of satisfaction. Often gathered through surveys or discussion groups, this type of data helps uncover perceptions of program effectiveness, organizational reputation, and community trust. While perceptual data is inherently subjective, collecting it at scale can reveal consistent themes that inform service improvement. For example, clients may express that while they are grateful for assistance, they often feel rushed or unheard during appointments—indicating a need to improve customer experience.

Qualitative data can be gathered through:

- **Surveys**: Open ended feedback from customers, staff, community members, and partners.

- **Focus Groups**: Facilitated discussions to uncover shared challenges or insights.

- **Interviews**: One-on-one conversations with stakeholders, including residents, board members, and elected officials.

- **Direct Observations**: Firsthand documentation of processes or community conditions.

Qualitative data provides the emotional and experiential depth that complements the clarity of numbers. When used alongside quantitative data, it paints a more complete picture—one that honors the voices of the people served and ensures decisions are shaped by both evidence and empathy.

Ensuring Data Quality and Reliability

The power of data lies in its quality. Without accurate, reliable, and comprehensive data, organizations cannot make informed decisions, and their ability to identify and address barriers is compromised. Poor-quality data—whether outdated, incomplete, or drawn from unreliable sources—creates a poor foundation that can lead to misguided strategies, wasted resources, and outcomes that fail to align with the organization's mission. Quality decisions require quality data, and the Navigation phase is where organizations must commit to this standard to ensure their efforts are both purposeful and effective.

"The power of data lies in its quality."

To achieve this, organizations must prioritize data that meets the following criteria:

- **Credible data** is drawn from trusted, verified sources, such as government reports, peer-reviewed research, and reputable studies. Internally, credibility depends on the accuracy of organizational records and reporting systems. Using credible data eliminates guesswork and builds confidence in the results, ensuring that decisions are grounded in evidence rather than speculation.

- **Timely data** reflects current conditions and trends. Outdated data distorts reality, making barriers appear more or less significant than they truly are. For example, relying on housing statistics from five years ago might overlook a recent housing crisis. Using up-to-date information ensures that the organization's understanding of barriers aligns with the present reality.

- **Comprehensive data** comes from multiple, diverse sources to provide a full, well-rounded view of the landscape. No single dataset can tell the whole story. Combining external sources like government statistics and community studies with internal organizational data —such as program outcomes or customer demographics —creates a clearer picture of the barriers that exist at both the individual and systemic levels.

- **Validated data** has been reviewed and analyzed by qualified professionals to ensure accuracy, consistency, and relevance. Even credible data can be misinterpreted if not carefully analyzed in context. Validation ensures the findings align with the organization's mission, helping leaders prioritize barriers that are both significant and actionable.

High-quality data not only meets these standards but also empowers organizations to make decisions that are data-driven— one of the core tenets of the *INSPIRE* framework. Data-driven decisions are not based on assumptions or anecdotal evidence; they are rooted in a careful analysis of measurable trends and human experiences, ensuring the identified barriers are both statistically significant and deeply relevant to the mission.

The Navigation phase is not simply about completing a research task; it is about ensuring the organization has the data it needs to make informed decisions that align with its mission and drive excellence. By committing to high-quality, validated data and combining measurable trends with meaningful human insights, organizations position themselves to make informed, impactful choices that move them closer to achieving their purpose.

THE COMMUNITY ASSESSMENT: UNDERSTANDING EXTERNAL FACTORS

The Community Assessment is a cornerstone of the Navigation phase, where organizations collect, analyze, and prioritize external factors that impact their ability to fulfill their mission. This process builds on the principles of high-quality, reliable data outlined in the previous section.

A successful Community Assessment does more than compile tables or present statistics—it tells a story. This is the story of the problem, its root causes, its impact on individuals and communities, and the opportunities available to address it. For the data to guide meaningful decisions, it must be carefully analyzed, contextualized, and prioritized. Findings should incorporate statistical trends, qualitative insights, and supporting evidence from external studies, academic research, and peer-reviewed sources. The result is a comprehensive understanding of external challenges—both personal and infrastructural—that affect individuals, families, and communities.

To make the findings accessible and actionable, we recommend organizing the Community Assessment into the following well-structured components:

Executive Summary

The executive summary serves as the high-level overview of the assessment. This section should highlight:

- Key trends and findings from the assessment.

- Prioritized barriers, ensuring that stakeholders clearly understand which challenges are the most pressing and impactful.

- Brief insights into strengths and opportunities that may support improvement efforts.

By providing a concise yet meaningful overview, the executive summary becomes an essential tool for engaging board members, funders, and other key decision-makers who may not need to dive into the full report.

Key Findings Report

The key findings report expands on the executive summary by offering a more detailed analysis of the primary insights. This section should highlight the most critical personal barriers (challenges in individuals' lives) and infrastructural barriers (systemic gaps in the community). Each barrier must be supported by data and analysis to establish its relevance and magnitude.

By combining qualitative insights with quantitative trends this section ensures the most impactful barriers are well-supported and understood.

Community Findings

For organizations that serve multiple communities, it is critical to recognize that barriers may differ across geographic areas. This section provides a localized breakdown of challenges and strengths, enabling organizations to tailor their strategies to targeted areas while contributing to a broader understanding of the entire service area. For example, one county may face barriers in the transportation infrastructure, while another county may show significant gaps in healthcare access. This section ensures no community is overlooked and reinforces the importance of localized solutions to systemic problems.

Regional Report

The regional report is the centerpiece of the Community Assessment. It brings together the most comprehensive analysis of the full service area by weaving together multiple sources of data into a unified narrative. This section moves beyond isolated statistics and instead tells the story of the region—its strengths, its challenges, and the conditions shaping the lives of those served.

- **Statistical Data**: This includes detailed quantitative analysis featuring multi-year trends, regional benchmarks,* and contextual narratives that explain why each data point matters. In alignment with the Mission Aligned Data Driven (MADD) mentality, statistical data should never stand alone—it must be connected to the organization's purpose. Each figure should be interpreted in light of the problem the organization is trying to solve.

  For example, if a community shows lower-than-average adult education attainment, the report for an antipoverty organization should reference research linking educational achievement to employment rates, average wages, and long-term poverty outcomes. By grounding these statistics in verified studies and directly tying them to the organization's mission, leaders can better understand the root causes of community needs—and make more intentional, informed decisions about where to focus resources.

---

* Comparing local data to state or national averages.

- **Community Feedback**: This includes qualitative data from surveys, interviews, and focus groups. Capturing stakeholder voices—residents, staff, board members, local leaders, and businesses—ensures that the quantitative data is grounded in lived experience. These insights provide nuance and emotional resonance, clarifying the "why" behind the numbers and helping prioritize the most urgent issues from a community perspective.

- **Agency Data**: This includes insights from the organization's own database, including customer demographics, service utilization trends, and populations most affected by the identified barriers. It allows organizations to connect external findings with internal performance and responsiveness, adding depth to the analysis. Agency data also helps identify gaps between community needs and service reach, supporting strategic planning.

- **Resource Inventory**: This component provides an overview of existing resources, partnerships, and service providers in the community. It helps identify where support systems are strong and where gaps exist. Highlighting opportunities for collaboration, innovation, or investment, this section supports a strategic understanding of how current assets can be leveraged—and where new efforts are needed—to address barriers and fulfill the mission.

Socioeconomic Research Domains:

To make the assessment findings actionable, the report should be organized into clearly defined domains. Domains group related indicators and trends into categories that reflect the key areas of life affected by the organization's mission. They serve as both an analytical framework and a communication tool—making it easier for stakeholders to understand the scope of the challenges, the connections between issues, and where solutions are most needed.

Each domain should include both strengths (existing assets, resources, or promising trends) and weaknesses (gaps, systemic barriers, or concerning patterns). This balance ensures the assessment is not just a list of problems, but a foundation for targeted, data-driven solutions. Community Action Agencies—and other organizations working to reduce poverty—may find the following domains useful for evaluating conditions in their communities:

- **Income:** Explore household income levels, distribution, and disparities across geographic and demographic groups. This domain offers critical insight into financial security, purchasing power, and economic mobility.

- **Employment:** Examine job availability, local industries, unemployment rates, and underemployment. Employment data reflects the region's economic stability and opportunities for upward mobility.

- **Adult Education:** Assess adult educational attainment levels such as high school completion, GED acquisition, literacy and numeracy limitations, and language barriers. This data can be tied directly to workforce readiness and long-term earnings potential.

- **Child/Youth Education:** Review academic performance, school attendance, dropout rates, graduation rates, and school performance. Educational achievement during formative years is a strong predictor of future socioeconomic outcomes.

- **Early Education and Childcare:** Analyze access to affordable, high-quality childcare and early childhood education. Gaps in availability or affordability often prevent parents from working and children from developing foundational skills.

- **Housing:** Address affordability, housing quality, homeownership rates, and homelessness. Stable housing is a foundational need, and housing insecurity often intersects with many other barriers.

- **Health:** Include data on physical and mental health outcomes, access to care, life expectancy, and behavioral health trends. Poor health limits employment opportunities and overall well-being.

- **Nutrition:** Examine food insecurity, access to healthy food, and participation in nutrition programs. Poor nutrition is often a result of systemic challenges and contributes to health and development issues.

- **Transportation:** Assess vehicle ownership, commute times, and public transportation infrastructures. Inadequate transportation options can limit access to jobs, healthcare, and education.

- **Family Relationships:** Explore indicators of family stability such as domestic violence, foster care, and multigenerational support systems. Family dynamics influence resilience and long-term success.

- **Community Engagement:** Include voting participation, community involvement, crime rates, veteran information, and volunteerism. High civic engagement often reflects community cohesion and empowerment, while low engagement may signal social isolation or disconnection.

Prioritizing Barriers: A Data Driven Process

The final step in the Community Assessment process is to prioritize the barriers identified throughout the report. While a wide range of challenges may emerge, not all carry the same level of urgency or strategic importance. For organizations committed to mission alignment and measurable impact, it becomes essential to determine which barriers deserve immediate focus, resource allocation, and strategic attention.

Although there are many valid approaches to prioritization, our firm has developed a methodology through years of experimentation that ensures balance, fairness, and purpose. We use a two-step data normalization* process that assigns equal weight to four distinct elements, each representing a critical lens through which barriers can be understood and compared:

- **Prevalence** reflects the number of people impacted, offering a population-level view of the issue based on hard data.

- **Perception** captures the number of survey respondents who identified the barrier as a top concern, amplifying community voice and perceived urgency.

---

* Converting different types of data (like percentages, counts, or ratios) into a common scale so they can be compared fairly. This helps ensure no single type of data dominates the analysis just because of how it's measured.

- **Experience** measures the number of people who report personally encountering the barrier, reflecting its day-to-day impact and relevance.

- **Accessibility** assesses the degree to which services exist to meet the need, revealing gaps between what people need and what the current infrastructure can support.

Each element tells a different part of the story. Prevalence helps quantify scale. Perception elevates the lived experiences and priorities of those closest to the work. Experience demonstrates how frequently barriers are encountered in real life. And accessibility shines a light on system-level shortfalls. By assigning equal weight to all four dimensions, no single perspective dominates the process—ensuring that prioritization reflects both evidence and empathy.

To ensure fairness across diverse data types, we use min-max normalization, a statistical method that allows different kinds of information—counts, percentages, and ratios—to be compared on equal footing. This process unfolds in two steps:

The first step is to rescale each data point to fall between 1 and 100 using the min-max normalization formula:

$$X_{normalized} = \left(\frac{(X - min)}{(max - min)} \right) \times 99 + 1$$

Here, X represents the raw score for a particular barrier, Min is the lowest score in that category across all barriers, and Max is the highest. Multiplying by 99 and adding 1 ensures that all scores fall on a scale from 1 to 100, eliminating zero as a potential output and preserving every barrier's visibility in the final score. A score of 1 represents the least severe case, while 100 reflects the most severe.

For example, imagine the number of people impacted by transportation issues ranges from 200 to 1,200 across different counties. If one county reports 700 people affected, the formula would produce a normalized prevalence score of approximately 52. This approach is repeated for all four dimensions—prevalence, perception, experience, and accessibility—resulting in four normalized scores per barrier.

This step ensures that no matter how the data was originally collected—whether as a percentage, a count, or a ratio—it is now comparable on the same scale, preserving fairness and accuracy in the comparison.

After all four scores have been normalized, they are summed together to produce a composite barrier score, with a total possible value ranging from 4 to 400. To bring this final total back into the same familiar range of 1 to 100, we normalize the composite scores one final time using the same min-max process.

This second round of normalization generates a final score for each barrier that reflects its overall significance based on all four dimensions equally. The result is a prioritized list that balances data with voice, systems with experience, and scope with urgency.

This method ensures that organizations are not simply reacting to the loudest concerns or the most readily available data. Instead, they are taking a comprehensive, structured, and equitable approach that reflects their commitment to data-driven, mission-aligned decision-making. By combining diverse forms of evidence into a single, unified process, the organization can move forward with clarity, focus, and integrity into the next phase of the *INSPIRE* framework: Strategy.

To enhance transparency and support stakeholder understanding, organizations can use data visualization tools to display their final prioritized scores. One particularly effective method is the Pareto chart, which ranks barriers in descending order of severity to show which issues account for the largest cumulative impact. Based on the 80/20 principle—suggesting that roughly 80% of effects stem from 20% of causes—Pareto charts often reveal that a small number of barriers contribute to the majority of the challenge. These visuals not only enhance data storytelling but also make it easier to communicate priorities with clarity to boards, funders, and the broader community.

ORGANIZATIONAL ASSESSMENT: EVALUATING INTERNAL FACTORS

The Organizational Assessment is a critical component of the Navigation phase, where organizations look inward to evaluate their internal operations, structures, and resources. While the Community Assessment identifies external barriers, this process ensures that the organization itself has the systems and capacity needed to respond effectively. Excellence is not achieved by chance; it requires alignment, efficiency, and intentional leadership at every level of the organization. By evaluating internal factors, organizations can identify gaps, inefficiencies, and opportunities for improvement, ensuring they are fully equipped to fulfill their mission.

A rigorous internal evaluation focuses on a variety of key areas that serve as the pillars of operational success. These areas are critical for any nonprofit organization striving for excellence and mission alignment. An example of the areas that should be evaluated is presented below:

1. Governance

Governance is the foundation of an effective organization, and the role of the board cannot be overstated. A well-structured, engaged, and skilled board ensures accountability, strategic direction, and oversight of the organization's mission and operations. The Organizational Assessment examines the following components of governance:

- **Board Size and Structure**: Boards should be appropriately sized and structured to allow for effective decision-making, diverse perspectives, and adequate representation. Too large a board can lead to inefficiencies, while too small a board may lack the capacity to provide sufficient oversight.

- **Skills and Expertise**: Boards should include members with diverse, relevant skills, including financial oversight, legal knowledge, fundraising, strategic planning, and an understanding of the mission. Regular skills assessments can help identify gaps and ensure the board evolves with the organization's needs.

- **Engagement**: An engaged board actively participates in meetings, provides strategic input, and advocates for the organization. Evaluating board attendance, committee participation, and fundraising involvement can reveal areas for improvement.

- **Bylaws and Policies**: Strong bylaws outline clear processes for board member selection, orientation, and, if necessary, removal. This ensures accountability and protects the integrity of the organization. Regular review of bylaws and governance policies ensures alignment with best practices.

- **Committee Structure**: Effective boards establish committees to address critical areas such as finance, governance, fundraising, and executive evaluation. Committees ensure that work is divided efficiently and that all aspects of governance receive adequate attention.

2. Leadership

Strong leadership drives organizational success. Leadership teams must be appropriately structured to support team members, promote a positive culture, and ensure that administrative tasks are executed effectively. Leadership must also model excellence, using data and mission alignment to guide decision-making. Key areas of focus include:

- **Size and Structure**: The leadership team should reflect the organization's size, scope, and needs. Roles must be clearly defined, ensuring that all critical administrative, strategic, and programmatic functions are covered.

- **Support for Team Members**: Effective leaders create an environment where team members feel supported. This includes providing professional development opportunities, regular feedback, and removing barriers that hinder performance. Leaders should be accessible and responsive to the needs of their teams.

- **Promoting Positive Culture**: Leadership sets the tone for organizational culture. Leaders must foster an environment of trust, respect, and collaboration where team members are inspired to perform at their best. A positive culture reduces turnover, improves morale, and enhances overall performance.

- **Skills and Engagement**: Leaders must possess the skills needed to align operations with the organization's mission. They should demonstrate financial acumen, data literacy, and strategic thinking while remaining deeply engaged in the organization's purpose and impact.

- **Data-Driven Decision-Making**: Strong leaders use high-quality data to inform their decisions, ensuring that strategies are effective, efficient, and mission-aligned. They establish systems for regularly reviewing performance metrics and making course corrections as needed.

3. Human Resources

The strength of any organization lies in its people. Human resources assessments focus on staffing levels, structure, morale, and the overall health of the workforce. Key areas to evaluate include:

- **Staffing Levels**: Adequate staffing is essential to meet organizational goals and maintain operational efficiency. Understaffing can lead to burnout, while overstaffing may strain financial resources.

- **Role Clarity and Structure**: Each team member must have a clearly defined role, with responsibilities that align with organizational goals. Overlapping roles or role confusion can lead to inefficiencies.

- **Morale and Engagement**: High staff morale leads to better performance and retention. Assessments should include surveys, interviews, or focus groups to evaluate job satisfaction, workload balance, and team culture.

- **Professional Development**: Investing in staff development ensures team members have the skills and tools they need to grow and succeed. This includes training, mentorship programs, and leadership development.

- **Policies and Procedures**: Strong HR policies ensure fair practices in hiring, onboarding, evaluation, and conflict resolution. Policies must comply with legal requirements and align with the organization's values.

4. Finance and Resource Management

Financial sustainability is a cornerstone of nonprofit excellence. Organizations must ensure transparency, sustainability, and strong financial controls. This evaluation examines:

- **Budgeting Processes**: Effective budgeting aligns resources with strategic priorities and ensures fiscal discipline. Budgets should be realistic, inclusive of all expenses, and adaptable to changing conditions.

- **Financial Reporting**: Regular, transparent financial reporting allows leadership and the board to monitor progress and make data-informed decisions.

- **Procurement Policies**: Strong policies ensure that resources are acquired responsibly and cost-effectively, minimizing waste and fraud.

- **Insurance and Risk Management**: Adequate insurance coverage protects the organization's assets, operations, and reputation. Risk management practices proactively address potential vulnerabilities.

- **Resource Allocation**: Resources must be allocated to maximize impact while maintaining sustainability. This includes assessing overhead costs, grant management processes, and funding diversification.

5. Operations (Strategy Implementation)

Operations are where strategy meets execution. This area evaluates the organization's ability to turn plans into measurable results while maintaining efficiency and effectiveness. Key considerations include:

- **Planning Processes**: Effective planning aligns short-term actions with long-term goals. Plans should include measurable targets, timelines, and accountability structures.

- **Efficiency and Effectiveness**: Organizations must continuously evaluate their processes to ensure services are delivered efficiently and resources are used effectively. Tools like Lean's Value Stream Mapping can identify inefficiencies and reduce waste.

- **Performance Tracking**: Regular monitoring of program and operational performance ensures the organization stays on course.

- **Accountability**: Clear systems for accountability ensure that team members understand their responsibilities and are equipped to deliver results.

6. Data and Analytics

Data drives informed decision-making, and organizations must ensure they have the processes, tools, and culture needed to collect, analyze, and use data effectively. Key areas of evaluation include:

- **Data Collection Systems**: The organization should have systems in place to collect data that is relevant, accurate, and aligned with its mission.

- **Quality Assurance**: Processes must exist to ensure data is reliable and up-to-date. Inaccurate data can lead to poor decisions and wasted resources.

- **Data Utilization**: Leadership and staff should use data to evaluate performance, identify trends, and make informed decisions.

- **Technology and Software**: Adequate technology and software systems support data collection, analysis, and reporting. Team members must be properly trained to use these tools effectively.

- **Actionable Insights**: Data analysis processes must translate findings into actionable strategies that inform planning and improvement efforts.

7. Capital (Facilities and Equipment)

Capital resources—such as facilities, vehicles, and equipment—must support the organization's operations and growth. Key areas include:

- **Facilities**: Buildings must be safe, functional, and provide adequate space for staff, volunteers, and customers. Insufficient or unsafe facilities can hinder productivity and create safety risks.

- **Vehicles and Equipment**: Vehicles and tools must be well-maintained and sufficient to support service delivery. For example, food banks require reliable trucks for deliveries, and housing organizations may need tools for repairs.

- **Scalability**: Facilities and equipment must accommodate current operations while allowing room for growth.

Investing in capital resources ensures the organization has the infrastructure needed to meet its operational and programmatic demands.

Bringing It Together

The Organizational Assessment shines a light on the internal strengths and weaknesses that influence an organization's ability to fulfill its mission. By evaluating key areas such as governance, leadership, staffing, financial systems, operations, data infrastructure, and physical capacity, organizations gain a clear understanding of where alignment exists—and where it must be improved. To support this evaluation, many organizations incorporate proven tools and methods that help diagnose inefficiencies, visualize workflows, and assess overall readiness. Techniques such as Lean's Value Stream Mapping, process mapping, and internal capacity diagnostics can surface bottlenecks and resource gaps, guiding improvement efforts with precision. These insights lay the groundwork for strategy development and ensure that internal systems are ready to support long-term impact.

FINAL THOUGHTS

The Navigation phase is about discovery—gaining clarity on the barriers, both external and internal, that affect your organization's ability to fulfill its mission. By using high-quality data to identify challenges and opportunities, you position your organization to make informed, mission-aligned decisions.

This phase does not solve problems but lays the groundwork for the strategies to come. With a comprehensive understanding of your landscape, you're now ready to move to the next phase: Strategy—where you will develop actionable plans to address barriers and achieve measurable outcomes.

It is important to recognize that these assessment processes—whether evaluating the community, your organization, or both—require a significant investment of time, expertise, and resources. Excellence in assessment often demands advanced skills and experience; organizations may benefit from hiring staff with a strong background in data analysis or engaging seasoned research consultants to ensure quality and rigor. This is not the place to cut corners. Without strong, well-designed assessments, an organization can never truly become data driven. Investing in thorough and honest assessment up front paves the way for fulfillment of your purpose, increases your likelihood of long-term success, and ensures that your strategies will be built on a solid foundation.

REFLECTION

Use the following questions to guide team discussion and deepen your understanding of the barriers and opportunities your organization faces:

- **Assess:** *Is your organization collecting and using the right types of quantitative and qualitative data to understand both internal and external barriers?*

- **Reflect:** *Have you accurately prioritized the most pressing challenges that impact your mission—and are those decisions informed by high-quality data?*

- **Act:** *Write down one step that you can take to improve the quality of your next community assessment.*

CHAPTER 7
STRATEGY

STRATEGY AS THE PINNACLE OF INSPIRE

Strategy is where intentionality meets accountability—the culmination of the *INSPIRE* framework and the stage where organizational aspirations are transformed into operational reality. In this phase, the insights uncovered during Navigation are converted into actionable strategies that are grounded in the organization's identity. Every initiative developed at this stage is informed by robust data, shaped by mission and vision, and designed to remove barriers with measurable, meaningful outcomes.

This is also the critical moment where organizations must determine which of the identified challenges should be addressed, can be addressed, and how best to take action. Not every barrier uncovered in the assessment phase will be within the organization's scope, capacity, or mission alignment to tackle directly. Strategy brings focus—turning a long list of potential priorities into a tightly aligned set of commitments.

While many organizations engage in strategic planning, their efforts too often result in documents that are disconnected from operations—plans that sit on shelves rather than shape day-to-day decisions. A true organization of excellence avoids this pitfall by designing a plan that meets three essential criteria: simplicity, actionability, and accountability. These principles ensure that the strategy becomes a living, breathing guide for impact—not just a formality, but a force.

Simplicity

One of the first questions we always ask a board during the organizational evaluation process is whether they know how to measure the success of their programs. On average, we find that only about 20% of governing body members can answer this question with clarity. This lack of shared understanding is not a minor oversight—it's a significant challenge. If board members are uncertain about how to evaluate success, how can the community understand it? How can stakeholders or funders be convinced to invest in the organization's work? A lack of clarity at the top creates a ripple effect of uncertainty that undermines trust, alignment, and credibility.

Simplicity addresses this issue head-on—not by removing substance, but by removing confusion. A simple plan ensures

STRATEGY

that success is defined, measurable, and communicated in a way that resonates with all stakeholders. By stripping away unnecessary complexity, organizations can clearly articulate their priorities and strategies, making them accessible to everyone—from board members to staff to external partners. Simplicity does not mean sacrificing depth or rigor; rather, it emphasizes precision and focus, enabling each individual to understand the organization's direction and their role in its success.

When presented in straightforward terms, a strategic plan allows board members to track progress, ask informed questions, and make data-driven decisions. Simplicity empowers them to recognize whether the organization is meeting its goals and, if not, to identify exactly where adjustments are needed.

This clarity extends beyond the boardroom. A simple plan fosters alignment across the organization, helping staff understand how their daily work contributes to larger goals. It also builds trust among community partners and stakeholders, who are more likely to invest in an organization that not only articulates its objectives but consistently demonstrates progress toward its mission.

Simplicity is not just a matter of good communication—it is a strategic advantage. By focusing on clear, measurable outcomes, organizations can cut through the noise and ensure that every effort is directed toward meaningful, mission-aligned impact.

Actionability

An actionable plan is what transforms the mission into motion—it bridges the gap between aspiration and execution. Without a clear path forward, even the most compelling goals can remain out of reach. Actionability ensures that strategies are not just words on a page, but fully formed programs and initiatives that drive results.

To be actionable, a strategy must be broken down into specific, measurable steps. Each step should clearly state what needs to be done, who is responsible, and the timeframe for completion. This level of clarity empowers staff and stakeholders to take ownership of their roles, aligning individual actions with the organization's broader objectives. It eliminates ambiguity, reduces inertia, and turns high-level goals into practical, day-to-day tasks.

Actionability also fuels momentum. When strategies are broken into achievable milestones, teams are more likely to see progress—and that progress reinforces engagement. Instead of waiting for distant, long-term results, organizations can celebrate incremental wins, course-correct in real time, and build a culture of forward motion.

Also, actionability provides structure for resource allocation. When the steps are clear, leaders can more easily determine what tools, training, funding, or partnerships are needed to bring the strategy to life. This enables the organization to act with focus and efficiency, rather than responding reactively or spreading resources too thin.

Ultimately, actionability is about operationalizing purpose. It ensures that bold ideas don't get lost in abstraction, but are grounded in work that can be tracked, managed, and improved. An actionable plan turns intention into implementation—and it is this transformation that makes the strategy real.

Accountability

A plan without accountability risks becoming little more than a wish list. Accountability ensures that each strategy is tracked, measured, and refined as necessary. By assigning ownership, establishing timelines, and defining clear performance indicators, organizations create mechanisms for oversight and evaluation. But accountability is more than a reporting function—it is a

STRATEGY

cultural commitment to transparency, performance, and growth. It ensures that progress is not assumed, but verified. It reinforces organizational discipline, builds credibility with funders and stakeholders, and fosters a work environment where individuals understand their role in delivering results. In this way, accountability transforms strategy from an idea into a shared responsibility—and from a document into a dynamic practice.

"A plan without accountability risks becoming little more than a wish list."

This chapter provides a comprehensive guide to developing a strategic plan that embodies these principles. From preparation and prioritization to the creation of actionable strategies and measurable outcomes, the following sections will equip organizations to craft a plan that is simple, actionable, and accountable. The goal is not merely to create a document but to establish a process that drives sustained, mission-driven impact.

PREPARATION

The first step to a successful strategy is preparation. Ensuring the right environment, resources, and tools are in place sets the tone for focused, productive work. The *INSPIRE* Committee, or designated planning team, should take steps to create an atmosphere conducive to collaboration and deep focus.

Begin by selecting a comfortable space that accommodates all participants. The environment should be well-lit, temperature-controlled, and equipped with functional chairs and workspaces. Provide snacks, drinks, and a catered lunch to keep energy levels high and minimize disruptions. Arrange seating so all participants can see the screen and flipcharts used during the process.

In terms of materials, provide planning packets summarizing key findings from the community and organizational assessments. These packets should include high-level data points, while full assessment documents remain available for reference. A well-structured slide deck should also guide discussions and ensure alignment throughout the session.

Finally, assign a skilled moderator—ideally a neutral, third-party consultant—to facilitate discussions. The moderator ensures focus, keeps the team aligned, and creates space for every voice to be heard.

THE PLANNING SESSION

Start by welcoming participants and introducing the purpose of the session. This ensures everyone understands their role, the importance of planning, and how the strategic plan will drive mission-aligned action. If regulatory or funding requirements influence the planning process, these should be reviewed at the beginning to set expectations.

All members of the team, including visiting consultants, should introduce themselves and then review the agenda, including breaks and meal times. Use this time to set a collaborative tone, perhaps with a brief icebreaker or a discussion of shared goals. This helps establish trust and encourages active participation.

Reviewing the Organizational Identity

Before diving into data and priorities, revisit the organization's identity—its mission, vision, values, and goals. This step ensures that all participants remain anchored to the principles that define the organization. The goal is not to change these elements but to use them as a lens through which strategies are developed. Alignment with identity ensures that every initiative contributes directly to the organization's overarching purpose.

Reviewing Family and Community Barriers

The first substantive step in planning is to review the key findings of the community assessment, focusing on barriers that impact individuals and families. These barriers, such as lack of affordable housing, limited transportation, or insufficient access to healthcare, represent personal and systemic challenges that require targeted interventions. Using quantitative data to outline the scope and scale of these issues and qualitative insights to highlight lived experiences ensures a comprehensive understanding of the challenges faced by the community.

Participants should explore these findings in depth, discussing their implications and how they align with the organization's identity. This review sets the stage for informed prioritization, ensuring that strategies are both impactful and actionable.

Selecting Family/Community Priorities

Once the barriers are reviewed, the next step is prioritization. While there are several valid approaches to narrowing down strategic focus, we typically recommend using a *priority consensus ranking* process. This method balances evidence with team insight, allowing organizations to elevate the barriers that are both critical and feasible to address.

Participants are asked to independently rank their top three barriers at the family and community levels, drawing on a mix of factors such as mission alignment, severity of impact, number of people affected, and the organization's current capacity to respond. Responses are collected using visual methods like tally sheets, sticky notes, colored dots, or live digital polling—depending on the session format.

Once individual selections are compiled, the group reviews the results together. Barriers that receive the highest number of votes are discussed in greater depth, including any differences in interpretation, urgency, or perceived solvability. This dialogue allows the team to clarify definitions, surface hidden insights, and ensure that final selections reflect both data and lived experience.

The goal is to arrive at a focused set of high-impact priorities that the organization can realistically address with its available resources. While the Community Assessment offers an initial data-informed ranking, this consensus step ensures that team perspectives and practical realities are fully considered. The result is a prioritized roadmap that's not only grounded in evidence, but also informed by organizational judgment and shared ownership.

STRATEGY

Developing Family/Community-Level Strategies

With priority barriers identified, the next step is to build strategies that are focused, outcome-oriented, and operationally clear. Each strategy should serve as a direct response to a specific barrier—grounded in the organization's mission and designed to drive measurable impact.

Rather than listing vague goals or broad service menus, each strategy must be constructed around a single, clearly defined outcome. This outcome becomes the primary measure of success and ensures shared understanding across leadership, staff, and partners. When outcomes are clear, resources can be targeted effectively, and progress can be evaluated with confidence.

While each strategy is designed to stand on its own, organizations should also recognize the interconnectivity of their work. In reality, many barriers are linked—improvements in one area (such as transportation or childcare) can have cascading effects on outcomes in employment, education, or health. During planning, leaders should also consider how customers served by one program can be connected to others to promote more holistic support and greater overall improvement. By designing strategies that align across programs, organizations create stronger referral pathways, reduce duplication, and maximize each customer's opportunity to succeed. This level of integration not only amplifies individual impact but also accelerates mission fulfillment.

Each strategy should include the following components:

- **Name:** A concise title that communicates the strategy's focus

- **Primary Barrier:** The core challenge the strategy is designed to eliminate or reduce

- **Primary Outcome:** A single, measurable result that defines successful removal of the barrier

- **Projected Enrollment:** The number of individuals or families expected to be served (Family Level)

- **Projected Success:** The number or percent expected to achieve the defined outcome

- **Timeline:** A schedule for implementation, including start/end dates for any key milestones

This structure transforms strategy from abstract intent into specific commitment. It clarifies who will be served, what change is expected, and when results should be achieved. When consistently applied, this approach strengthens alignment, sharpens accountability, and ensures that every strategy moves the organization closer to its mission.

Reviewing the Organizational Assessment

The second half of the strategic planning session turns the organization's focus inward. While the Community Assessment examines external barriers, the Organizational Assessment

STRATEGY

provides a mirror—inviting the agency to examine its internal capacity, systems, and structures. This phase of the process ensures that the strategies developed are not only mission-aligned, but also feasible, given the organization's current reality.

The review begins with a careful examination of findings from the Organizational Assessment. This includes feedback from internal stakeholders—staff, board members, and volunteers—often gathered through surveys or focus groups. These insights are paired with perspectives from customers, partners, and other community stakeholders, which may have been collected during the Community Assessment. Together, these voices paint a picture of how the organization is experienced, both internally and externally.

In addition to stakeholder input, the assessment draws from a review of organizational documents such as bylaws, audits, budgets, strategic plans, policies, and internal reports. These materials help contextualize how the agency operates—financially, structurally, and culturally. By weaving together human insight and operational data, the assessment allows the planning team to evaluate how well the organization is positioned to achieve its mission and respond to community needs.

As the team begins to engage with the data, it is important to invite open reflection. Lived experiences from team members often add nuance and insight that may not be visible in the documents or survey results alone. This is an opportunity to build shared understanding and surface questions or tensions that may shape the direction of the plan.

After this open reflection, the planning team can begin analyzing the findings more formally. To support this process, we've developed tools that expand upon traditional approaches to organizational evaluation. These methods help the team organize their insights, identify strengths and vulnerabilities, and assess internal and external influences in a structured, mission-aligned way. These tools also support prioritization—allowing the organization to focus on the most urgent capacity-building opportunities with clarity and purpose

In the following sections, we'll explore these tools in greater detail and walk through how they can be applied to support effective strategic planning.

Evaluating Factors in the Organization's Control

To organize and assess the internal conditions that impact success, we use a structured evaluation process focused on factors within the organization's control. This process examines major operational areas—such as leadership, governance, staffing, finances, data systems, and facilities—and categorizes elements under each based on its current state.

This approach builds upon traditional *SWOT analysis* by replacing generalized labels like "strengths" and "weaknesses" with more precise categories. Each area is assigned to one of five classifications:

- **Excellence:** The organization demonstrates exceptional performance in this area, often setting an example for peers or the field. These areas are not just strong—they define the organization's reputation and serve as models for best practice.

- **Growth:** Positive change is evident, and the organization is actively improving. These areas show promise and forward momentum but have not yet reached full maturity or stability.

- **Complacency:** These areas may have been strengths in the past, but the organization has failed to maintain or expand upon previous success. Left unaddressed, complacency often leads to underperformance or missed opportunities.

- **Risk:** These areas expose the organization to significant threats—legal, financial, reputational, or operational. If not mitigated, risk can result in lawsuits, injury, loss of trust, or serious disruption to services.

- **Non-Compliance:** The organization is out of alignment with legal, regulatory, or funder requirements—even if these violations have not yet been flagged externally. Non-compliance is a critical concern, as it compromises eligibility, integrity, and long-term sustainability.

By applying this framework during the strategic planning session, organizations gain a clear picture of their operational landscape—identifying what is working, what needs development, and where urgent action is required.

Identifying Uncontrollable Factors

Mission-driven organizations operate in environments filled with uncertainty, complexity, and change. While they may have strong systems and leadership, there are always factors beyond their control that can either support or hinder their work. To maximize their effectiveness, organizations must be prepared to respond to, or take advantage of, these influences to the greatest degree possible. The goal is to make the achievement of the mission as easy and unobstructed as possible. That's where the *SPECTRAL* analysis comes in.

MISSION ALIGNED.DATA DRIVEN.

SPECTRAL stands for *Social (or Cultural), Political, Environmental, Community Engagement, Technological, Resource Availability, Accessibility, and Legal.* These eight categories form a comprehensive framework for assessing the broader environment in which the organization operates. This tool, developed specifically for mission-aligned organizations, builds upon and expands traditional scanning models like PESTEL, offering a more relevant and inclusive structure for community-focused work.

This process is not about forecasting the future—it's about understanding the present with enough clarity to anticipate opportunity, mitigate risk, and make informed decisions that keep the path to mission achievement as clear as possible. Here's how each element of *SPECTRAL* contributes to that understanding:

- **Social (or Cultural):** What cultural dynamics, belief systems, or social trends are influencing the community? This includes evolving family structures, generational shifts, language diversity, religious influence, or changing community expectations. For example, shifts in values related to work-life balance or equity may impact how programs are perceived or accessed.

- **Political:** What political dynamics—local, state, or national—could influence funding, policy, or public sentiment? This includes partisan divides, advocacy campaigns, elections, and political appointments that affect regulations, partnerships, or public engagement.

- **Environmental:** How are environmental conditions affecting your service area? This might include natural disasters, climate change, pollution, infrastructure degradation, or geographic isolation. These factors often intersect with issues like housing stability, public health, and access to basic needs.

- **Community Engagement:** What trends exist in civic participation, volunteerism, or public trust? Are residents showing increased or decreased involvement in local initiatives, voting, or nonprofit partnerships? High engagement can signal readiness for collaboration, while disengagement may require trust-building strategies.

- **Technological:** What advances or disruptions in technology might influence service delivery or operations? This includes new digital platforms, data systems, artificial intelligence, cybersecurity risks, or technology access disparities that may affect clients and staff alike.

- **Resource Availability:** What shifts are occurring in the availability of key resources, such as funding, workforce capacity, or donated goods? This includes changes in grant opportunities, labor shortages, inflation-driven cost increases, or competition for limited supplies.

- **Accessibility:** What barriers are emerging—or worsening—that limit equitable access to services? These may include transportation gaps, internet availability, physical infrastructure, disability accommodations, or language access. These challenges often prevent individuals from fully engaging with available supports.

- **Legal:** What legal frameworks, regulations, or court rulings are shaping the nonprofit sector or your service area? This may involve changes in employment law, data privacy requirements, contract compliance, or rulings that affect the rights of the populations you serve.

Each of these categories invites organizations to ask, *"What's happening around us that we need to understand—so we can respond with clarity, courage, and alignment to our mission?"*

Mapping Influence: The EASCU Analysis

After identifying key trends and conditions through the *SPECTRAL* process, organizations must go a step further: they must evaluate how each factor might influence their mission and operations. This is where the *EASCU* analysis comes in.

EASCU stands for *Empower, Advance, Sustain, Challenge, and Undermine*. These five categories represent different types of influence that a condition or trend may have on an organization. Unlike traditional models that simply list opportunities and threats, the *EASCU* framework allows for a more nuanced understanding—one that respects the complexity of operating in mission-driven environments.

This analysis doesn't just help identify what's happening. It clarifies how each condition could shape the organization's response.

- **Empower:** These are catalytic forces—conditions that could significantly accelerate the organization's ability to achieve its mission. Empowering influences often include game-changing opportunities, such as major funding expansions, influential partnerships, or community movements that directly align with the organization's purpose. For example, if a city announces a multi-year initiative to reduce child poverty, and your organization already operates in that space, this alignment can dramatically boost your impact and visibility.

- **Advance:** These influences support incremental progress. They may not change the game entirely, but they create forward movement. Examples include modest policy changes that increase flexibility in service delivery, new research that validates your approach, or moderate increases in community engagement. These elements help maintain momentum and support growth, even if they aren't transformative on their own.

- **Sustain:** Some conditions help hold the line. They preserve stability and continuity, ensuring that the organization can maintain current levels of service and effectiveness. These might include reliable funding from long-term partners, consistent board engagement, or steady public support. While not forward-moving forces, these influences are critical in preventing regression or disruption.

- **Challenge:** These are conditions that introduce obstacles—barriers that will require strategic workarounds or mitigation plans. These might include shifting client needs, increased service demand without a corresponding budget increase, or new regulatory requirements that strain internal systems. Challenges do not necessarily threaten the mission directly, but they demand attention and adaptation.

- **Undermine:** These are serious threats—conditions that could fundamentally weaken the organization's ability to fulfill its mission. Examples include the potential loss of a core funding stream, significant political opposition to key services, or damaging public narratives that erode trust. Undermining forces may not always be immediate, but if left unaddressed, they can disrupt operations or damage long-term sustainability.

Each *SPECTRAL* element should be evaluated using the *EASCU* lens. For instance, a shift in local government leadership (Political) may empower your work if the new administration is aligned with your mission—or it could challenge it if priorities diverge. A technology upgrade (Technological) may advance internal efficiency, while a rising digital divide (Accessibility) could undermine equitable service delivery.

By pairing environmental scanning with strategic classification, the *EASCU* process turns information into insight. It not only helps you understand what's changing—it helps you act on it. This structured evaluation guides the team in identifying which factors demand immediate strategic response, which offer new possibilities, and which require monitoring over time.

Selecting Organizational Priorities

While strategy development at the family and community levels focuses on external barriers affecting individuals and neighborhoods, agency-level strategies require a shift in perspective. Here, the goal is to identify and address internal conditions that limit the organization's ability to operate effectively, serve clients equitably, or achieve long-term sustainability.

The planning team begins by reviewing the organizational assessment findings—specifically, the results of the *EGCRN* and *EASCU* analyses. These tools help clarify which operational challenges are most urgent, most threatening, or most likely to create meaningful impact if addressed.

To select the barriers that the organization will focus on, committee members can use the same consensus ranking process described in the family/community section—or a similar method adapted for agency-level decision-making. Planning team members independently select the top three internal barriers they believe are most critical to address, considering mission alignment, organizational risk, operational impact, and capacity for change. These rankings are then compiled, discussed, and refined as a group, ensuring that the final selections reflect both organizational insight and practical feasibility.

Before jumping into strategy development, planning teams may also apply a simple Five Whys process to their top-ranked issues. This technique involves asking "why?" multiple times—typically five—to dig beneath surface symptoms and reveal the root cause. In doing so, teams often discover that meaningful change may require action at several layers of the problem, not just the final answer.

In alignment with Hoshin Kanri and other proven methodologies —including OKRs (Objectives and Key Results), 4DX (The 4

Disciplines of Execution), and Agile—we recommend limiting organizational priorities to no more than five at a time. These models, though varied in execution, share a central tenet: concentrated focus accelerates impact. When organizations attempt to address too many internal initiatives at once, momentum is lost, accountability fades, and strategic clarity gives way to operational chaos. A focused set of priorities, on the other hand, ensures that resources are directed where they matter most, attention remains undivided, and measurable progress is more likely to occur. This level of discipline is foundational to the MADD/*INSPIRE* approach, helping teams stay aligned and energized around the work that will generate the most meaningful improvement.

This prioritization also creates space for sustainable growth. By limiting strategies to a manageable number, each receives the time, energy, and oversight needed to succeed. Milestones can be clearly tracked, adjustments made in real time, and early wins celebrated—reinforcing progress and strengthening buy-in across the organization. Once a strategy has been fully implemented or embedded into daily operations, a new priority can be introduced, continuing the cycle. This rolling approach supports long-term transformation without overwhelming staff or compromising quality. Whether the focus is on strengthening leadership, upgrading data systems, or improving internal communication, this intentional pacing helps ensure that organizational strategies are not just launched—they are lived.

Developing Agency-Level Strategies

Once internal priorities have been selected, the planning team develops corresponding agency-level strategies using the same structured approach applied to family and community-level strategies. This ensures consistency across the strategic plan and

STRATEGY

reinforces alignment between organizational improvement efforts and external impact goals.

Each strategy should clearly identify the internal barrier it addresses, include a defined primary outcome, and outline an implementation timeline. By applying the same rigorous design process used for community-focused strategies, the organization ensures that internal efforts are equally focused, measurable, and aligned with the overall mission.

Developing Action Plans

With strategies now defined at the family, community, and agency levels, the final step is to develop detailed action plans. These plans serve as blueprints for execution—turning strategy into step-by-step action with assigned responsibility, timelines, and accountability measures.

Strategy Name						
Start Date:	Projected End Date:		Owner:			Actual Success
Need/Barrier:					Level (F/A/C):	F
Date Verified:	Need/Barrier Identification Method:			Domain:		
Strategic Goal:						
Primary Outcome:						
Projected Enrollment:	Projected Success:		Measurement Tool(s):			
Action Items (Service/Activity)			Responsible Party		Target Date	Status
Need/Barrier Narrative: *Why is the organization operating this strategy?*						
Description: *Who are the customers? How are they identified, solicited, enrolled, served, tracked? What financial/other resources will used for implementation?*						
Budget:	Sources:		Software:			
Admin Staff:	Service Staff:	Buildings:	Admin Vehicles:		Service Vehicles:	

Sample SA Howell, LLC Action Plan

MISSION ALIGNED.DATA DRIVEN.

Each action plan* begins by reaffirming the strategy's name, primary barrier, and primary outcome. From there, the following components are developed:

- **Action Steps**: The specific services or activities that will be delivered to achieve the strategy's outcome. In family-level strategies, these steps typically represent the core services provided to participants. Each action step should be clearly defined, realistically scoped, and directly tied to the removal of the identified barrier.

- **Responsible Parties**: Each action step should include the position, department, or partner responsible for carrying it out.

- **Timelines**: Each step should include its own target date for completion, reflecting the varying timeframes needed for true implementation. This ensures accountability across the full span of the strategy.

- **Key Performance Indicators (KPIs)**: Although the primary measurement of success for each strategy should have been previously selected, these supporting metrics allow for the tracking of incremental progress and secondary impacts.

- **Measurement Tools**: The systems, reports, or instruments that will be used to verify and validate both KPIs and the primary outcome. These tools must be relevant, reliable, and integrated into regular performance monitoring.

---

* For additional resources and a downloadable action plan template, visit sahowellco.com/document-library.

When designed effectively, action plans create clarity at every level of the organization. They identify what will be done, who is doing it, when it will be completed, and how success will be tracked. This structure moves strategy from promise to practice —and ensures that impact is not only envisioned, but achieved.

FINALIZING AND PRESENTING THE STRATEGIC PLAN

The finalized strategic plan should be presented in a polished, professional format that is easy to navigate and accessible to all stakeholders. Each section of the document should be logically structured, beginning with an executive summary that provides a high-level overview of the plan, including its purpose, key barriers addressed, and the strategies developed. Following this, the plan should include dedicated sections for family, community, and agency-level strategies, clearly delineated to provide a comprehensive view of the organization's approach.

Each strategy should be formatted consistently, specifying the barrier it addresses, the strategic actions planned, the primary measurement of success, additional key performance indicators (KPIs), and a detailed timeline for implementation. This ensures clarity and allows all stakeholders to easily understand the objectives and outcomes associated with each initiative.

Visual elements, such as charts, graphs, and infographics, can also be included to enhance comprehension and engagement. These tools can effectively convey complex data, highlight priorities, and showcase progress metrics in a way that resonates with diverse audiences. The use of these visual aids should complement the narrative, ensuring the plan remains accessible and impactful.

Finally, presenting the strategic plan in both print and digital formats allows for broad distribution and ease of access. This dual format ensures that the plan can reach a variety of audiences, including board members, staff, funders, and community partners. A well-designed document reflects the organization's professionalism and dedication to its mission, inspiring confidence and alignment among all stakeholders involved in implementing the strategies outlined.

BOARD REVIEW AND APPROVAL

Once the strategic plan has been finalized, it must be presented to the organization's governing body for review and approval. This step is crucial to ensure alignment with the entity's identity, as well as to secure the leadership's full support for implementation. During the review process, board members should critically evaluate whether the plan's targets and outcomes are achievable within the proposed timelines and with the available resources. They should also ensure that the strategies are directly aligned with the organization's purpose and long-term goals.

The review process offers an opportunity for refinement, allowing the governing body to provide valuable feedback that enhances the plan's effectiveness and feasibility. Securing board approval not only affirms organizational alignment but also establishes a clear mandate for action, reinforcing accountability across all levels of the organization.

ONGOING MONITORING AND ACCOUNTABILITY

A strategic plan reaches its full potential only when it becomes a living document—actively guiding decisions, actions, and performance across the organization. To achieve this, the plan must be integrated into the organization's regular review processes, ensuring that progress is monitored consistently and that results are used to inform real-time decision-making.

At each scheduled board meeting, progress toward the plan's primary outcomes and Key Performance Indicators (KPIs) should be reviewed. Strategy owners should provide structured updates on what has been achieved, where challenges have emerged, and what course corrections may be necessary to stay on track. These discussions turn planning into governance and help the board fulfill its role as a strategic steward.

To support this continuous accountability, each strategy should be documented in a scorecard, dashboard, or project management system that enables real-time tracking. These tools provide a visual, up-to-date overview of progress, making it easy to assess whether action steps are being completed on schedule, whether outcomes are being met, and whether additional support or adjustments are needed. A well-designed scorecard can highlight timelines, responsible parties, service delivery milestones, and key performance metrics—all in a format that promotes transparency and shared understanding.

Importantly, scorecards and dashboards should not be seen as reporting requirements—they are performance management tools. When integrated into regular board meetings, staff check-ins, and leadership reviews, these tools make the strategic plan tangible. They help ensure that it is not relegated to a binder or desktop file, but actively shapes the organization's culture, operations, and outcomes.

By embedding the strategic plan into ongoing organizational practices—and by equipping teams with the right tools to track progress—the plan becomes more than a roadmap. It becomes a dynamic force for continuous alignment, decision-making, and measurable impact.

FINAL THOUGHTS

The strategic planning process represents far more than the creation of a document—it is the blueprint for achieving the organization's purpose. Each strategy developed should not only address the barriers identified but also inspire confidence among stakeholders, empowering the organization to make meaningful, mission-driven progress.

As the organization advances through the INSPIRE framework, the strategy phase serves as the critical bridge between identifying challenges and achieving results. By prioritizing intentionality, accountability, and alignment, this phase lays the groundwork for effective execution, performance monitoring, and continuous improvement—bridging the gap between insight and impact.

REFLECTION

Discuss these questions with your team to ensure a clear understanding of the strategic planning process:

- **Assess**: *Does your current strategic plan clearly align with your organizational identity and the barriers identified during the Navigation phase?*

- **Reflect**: *In what ways might your plan fall short in terms of simplicity, actionability, or accountability—and how could that affect implementation?*

- **Act**: *Write down one specific enhancement you can make to improve your next strategic plan.*

CHAPTER 8
PERFORMANCE

WHERE PREPARATION MEETS THE MOMENT

Before I ever marched onto a football field in uniform, I had already performed each song a thousand times in my mind.

As a high school trombone player, I didn't just show up to rehearsal—I lived it. I practiced for hours every day—making sure that every note, every step, every transition was muscle memory.

My house sat on a hill overlooking the stadium, and I would often walk down alone just to rehearse on the field in the silence, visualizing where I'd be during each phrase of the music. I wanted it to feel so natural that when the moment came, I wouldn't have to think—I'd just perform.

And that's the heart of this chapter.

In the Mission Aligned Data Driven (MADD) framework, performance is where preparation meets the moment. It's not a one-time event, but the daily execution of strategy—where plans become action, and action becomes impact. Performance is not just a measure of outcomes—it's a reflection of culture, discipline, leadership, and the embodiment of preparation. It's what the world sees, regardless of how much work happened behind the scenes. The audience doesn't watch rehearsals. They watch the performance.

This phase of the *INSPIRE* framework asks a critical question: *Can your organization deliver?* Not just once—but consistently, reliably, and in real time. That kind of performance doesn't happen by accident. It takes systems that support follow-through, leaders who model discipline, and a team that is aligned and ready. Like a band on the field, it only works when everyone knows their part, trusts the process, and stays in sync with the rhythm of the work.

What we'll explore in this chapter isn't just how to track performance—it's how to build it. How to stay on course, adjust when needed, use feedback to improve, and lead with enough clarity and conviction to keep everyone moving in the right direction. Because in the end, no matter how brilliant the plan, performance is where it all comes to life.

STAY ON TARGET

Performance isn't just about movement—it's about movement with direction. A team can be busy, active, and constantly in motion, but still headed nowhere if it's not moving with clarity and intention. That's why, in this phase of the *INSPIRE* framework, one of the most essential disciplines is focus.

There's a moment in Star Wars: A New Hope that sticks with me every time I think about leadership under pressure. Rebel pilots are under fire, racing down the trench of the Death Star, and one pilot keeps repeating a quiet but urgent command: "Stay on target… stay on target." It's not just a line for dramatic effect—it's a principle. The goal is clear. The distractions are real. The

PERFORMANCE

stakes are high. And yet, the mission demands that you hold the line and focus on what matters most.

Distractions are a daily reality in mission-driven work. A last-minute request from a funder. A loud voice in a community meeting. A shiny new idea with vague alignment. It's easy to get pulled off course—not because of negligence, but because of noble intent applied in too many directions. When that happens, organizations don't just lose focus—they drift.

We talk often about mission drift—when a well-meaning organization starts serving objectives that no longer match its core purpose. But what we don't talk about enough is strategy drift—when a team, mid-implementation, slowly veers away from the very plan they worked so hard to build. Left unchecked, these small diversions compound over time. Energy is drained. Resources are scattered. Momentum is lost. And just like mission drift, strategy drift can feel harmless at first—until you look up and realize you're no longer headed in the direction you intended.

> "What we don't talk about enough is strategy drift - when a team, mid-implementation, slowly veers away from the very plan they worked so hard to build."

That's why strong leadership is essential during the performance phase. Leaders are the traction keepers. They're the ones responsible for keeping the organization connected to the plan and holding the line between vision and action. Because when traction is lost—even the best ideas stall.

In his book *How to Lead in a World of Distractions,* Clay Scroggins breaks down the word "distraction" in a way that's hard to forget. He reminds us that distraction literally means dis-traction —a loss of traction.[1]

Without traction, even the most powerful engine can't move. It doesn't matter how good your strategy is, or how fired up your team might be. If there's no grip on the ground, you're stuck.

He goes on to describe an event that many in the South remember vividly: *"Snowmageddon"*. In January 2014, the city of Atlanta was hit by what seemed like a minor winter storm— just a couple of inches of snow. But it paralyzed the entire metro area. Thousands of drivers were stranded on highways overnight. Children were stuck in schools. Emergency responders couldn't get where they needed to go. The issue wasn't the snowfall—it was the loss of traction. Once the wheels started spinning, progress became impossible. And with so many people all slipping at once, the whole system locked up.

Reading Clay's words reminded me of a lesson from my dad. Early in my driving years, he taught me how to control a vehicle in snow. I still remember him saying, "Don't fight the slide. Turn into it." When the car started to drift, he didn't want me to panic. He wanted me to adjust—just enough—to keep moving forward. That lesson wasn't just about driving. It was about leadership.

Staying on target doesn't mean ignoring change. It doesn't mean clinging rigidly to the original path, no matter what. It means maintaining control while embracing motion. It means recognizing the slide and steering with purpose. When traction feels weak, the instinct is often to slam on the brakes—but sometimes the answer is to lean in, correct gently, and keep moving.

That's what strategy-driven performance requires. Not a perfect road, but the skill and discipline to drive it well.

CREATING FEEDBACK LOOPS

Sustainable performance isn't just about execution—it's about reflection, adjustment, and shared ownership. That's why the most effective organizations don't just implement strategies; they create structured systems for communicating and refining them. In the language of Hoshin Kanri, this process is called *"Catchball"*—a dynamic exchange where ideas are passed back and forth between leaders and frontline staff, between departments and governing bodies, until everyone has had a chance to shape the strategy and commit to its success.

When strategy becomes conversation, alignment becomes culture.

Catchball transforms the strategic plan from a top-down directive into a collaborative process. It recognizes that those doing the work often hold critical insights about what's working, what's not, and what needs to change. Staff members are not just implementers—they're partners in performance. Through regular check-ins, team discussions, supervisor meetings, and planning reviews, organizations can establish feedback loops that elevate those insights to decision-makers in real time.

However, feedback doesn't just flow upward. Leaders must also share performance data, resource updates, and emerging decisions transparently with the team. This two-way communication builds trust, keeps everyone aligned, and reinforces a culture of accountability. When team members see how their feedback shapes direction—and how decisions are tied to strategy—they are more likely to stay engaged and motivated.

Effective feedback loops also extend beyond staff. Community partners, local officials, and even customers should have structured opportunities to offer input, raise concerns, and suggest course corrections. Whether through surveys, focus groups, advisory councils, or quarterly strategy updates, organizations can ensure their performance is informed by the perspectives of those they serve.

Ultimately, creating feedback loops isn't just about gathering opinions for the sake of inclusion. It's about strengthening execution through shared learning, responsive leadership, and adaptive strategy. A plan that can't adapt to feedback isn't a plan—it's a liability. But a plan that evolves in response to honest insight? That's performance in action.

Strong feedback loops allow teams to listen—but listening means little without something clear and meaningful to listen to. That's where data enters the equation.

TRACKING THE RIGHT DATA

In a Mission Aligned Data Driven organization, data is more than a reporting requirement—it's a strategic asset. It tells the story of what's working, what's not, and where the organization needs to go next. When performance falters, it's often not because of poor strategy, but because the right information wasn't available—or wasn't trusted—at the right time. This is why tracking the right data is essential.

Data-driven decision-making (DDDM) requires organizations to move beyond collecting data for compliance and instead focus on collecting data for insight. Meeting funding or regulatory requirements is important, but if that's the only reason data is collected, it becomes a checkbox exercise. True DDDM asks deeper questions: *Do we have the information we need to make timely, informed decisions? Can our staff and leadership understand what's happening and why? Are we tracking outcomes—or just outputs?*

To answer these questions, organizations must be intentional about the data they collect and how they collect it. Every data point should serve a purpose. Performance data should align with strategic goals, reflect key outcomes, and be actionable. This means designing systems that capture not only who was served or what service was provided, but also how clients progressed, where interventions were effective, and which approaches need refinement.

However, even the best-designed data systems fail without accuracy. Incomplete records, inconsistent definitions, and delayed entry all contribute to a distorted picture of performance. When data lacks integrity, it erodes trust. Leaders hesitate to use it. Staff lose motivation to maintain it. And ultimately, the strategic plan becomes harder to manage, monitor, and improve.

To avoid this, data collection processes must be built into daily operations—not as an afterthought, but as a core responsibility. Clear definitions, standardized procedures, and regular quality checks are essential. So is training. Everyone involved in data entry or analysis must understand why their work matters—and how it drives results.

Organizations should also ensure that data systems are user-friendly and aligned with real-world workflows. If collecting data becomes a burden or distraction, quality will suffer. But when systems are intuitive and aligned with mission outcomes, data becomes part of the performance culture—not an obstacle to it.

At this stage of the INSPIRE framework, data is no longer hypothetical. It becomes a daily performance tool—it helps staff stay focused, gives leaders insight, and ensures that mid-course corrections are based on reality—not assumptions.

Effective performance tracking also reveals how strategies interact and influence one another. Improvements in one area often produce ripple effects in others. For example, stronger transportation access may boost attendance in workforce programs, while wellness initiatives can increase staff focus and case management quality. Recognizing these interdependencies helps organizations coordinate efforts across departments, adjust strategies in real time, and amplify collective impact.

COURSE CORRECTION AND CONTINUOUS IMPROVEMENT

No plan—no matter how well designed—unfolds exactly as expected. That's why strategic performance isn't about executing perfectly; it's about learning constantly. Course correction is not a failure of planning—it's a sign that the organization is responsive, data-driven, and committed to doing what works.

The *INSPIRE* framework recognizes that strategy must be flexible enough to adapt as new information becomes available. But adaptation should never be reactionary. Continuous improvement requires intentionality. It means using data not just to track progress, but to ask critical questions: *Are we seeing the outcomes we anticipated? Are we allocating our resources effectively? Are our strategies resonating with those we serve?*

This feedback loop is powered by data, but it is fueled by reflection. Organizations must regularly create structured opportunities to review performance—whether through quarterly reports, standing strategy sessions, or dedicated team check-ins. In these forums, the goal isn't to justify past decisions—it's to improve future ones. Leaders should be prepared to adjust timelines, shift resources, or refine strategies based on what the data reveals.

Importantly, course correction doesn't always mean making large, sweeping changes. Sometimes it's a small tweak to a workflow, a reallocation of staff time, or a shift in outreach tactics. These micro-adjustments, made consistently and thoughtfully, are often what drive long-term results. And because they're grounded in data, they avoid the trap of chasing new trends or solving problems that don't exist.

This iterative mindset must be shared across the organization. Teams need to feel safe acknowledging when something isn't working—and empowered to suggest improvements. Leadership sets the tone here. When performance conversations are framed around learning and growth—not blame—they foster a culture of candor, curiosity, and collaboration.

The same mindset applies to data itself. Continuous improvement also means refining how performance is measured. *Are the current KPIs still the best indicators of success? Are new patterns emerging that weren't previously tracked?* Organizations should treat their KPIs as living tools, updating and refining them as new patterns emerge to keep performance management relevant and actionable.

Ultimately, the goal of course correction is not to steer away from the strategic plan—but to stay aligned with it more effectively. The best organizations hold tightly to their mission but remain flexible in their approach—listening to their data, trusting their people, and continuously evolving in service of impact.

SUSTAINING PERFORMANCE THROUGH MENTAL WELLNESS

A high-performing organization cannot exist without healthy people. As teams move from planning into full-scale implementation, the physical, emotional, and mental well-being of staff becomes not just a Human Resources concern, but a performance issue. Strategy cannot be executed at scale by teams that are depleted, distracted, or running on empty. If people are the engine of progress, then mental wellness is the fuel—and that fuel must be replenished intentionally and consistently.

Left unaddressed, fatigue doesn't just reduce productivity—it clouds judgment, slows decision-making, and increases the likelihood of drift. When people are worn down, it becomes harder to prioritize, easier to overreact, and more difficult to hold the line. In that way, mental exhaustion can quietly erode traction, sending even the best strategies into a slow slide away from impact.

The past few years have placed extraordinary stress on the workforce. The long shadow of the COVID-19 pandemic, ongoing economic instability, and growing uncertainty about the future of public funding have created conditions that heighten anxiety and emotional fatigue. Staff are often tasked with solving complex social problems while navigating their own personal stressors, all within systems that are stretched thin. In such an environment, burnout is not just possible—it's highly likely.

Forward-looking organizations are responding by embedding wellness into the fabric of operations. One increasingly effective approach involves the use of certified mental wellness coaches—trained professionals who help staff process stress, build resilience, and maintain emotional equilibrium. Whether through individual coaching, team-based sessions, or informal check-ins, these professionals offer a layer of support that reinforces psychological safety and long-term engagement.

Equally important are the physical spaces that support wellness. Some organizations have introduced exercise rooms that staff can use before or after work, or even during breaks. Others have added wellness rooms—quiet, dedicated spaces for rest, reflection, or mental reset. These facilities do more than offer convenience—they signal a cultural shift. When staff see that their health is valued not just in words but in physical infrastructure, it builds trust and encourages sustainable habits.

Workplace flexibility is another powerful tool. Allowing staff to adjust their hours, work remotely, or tailor their schedules provides a sense of autonomy and control—two essential elements of emotional well-being. In high-stress environments, even small degrees of flexibility can reduce tension, increase retention, and improve performance.

Finally, organizations must foster a culture where mental wellness is talked about openly. Leaders set the tone. When they model transparency about stress and self-care—and encourage staff to do the same—they create a workplace where support is not just available but expected. Mental health becomes part of the organizational conversation, not a sidebar.

A thriving mission requires a thriving workforce. By investing in wellness infrastructure, supporting staff with trained professionals, and embedding flexibility and openness into the culture, organizations can protect one of their most valuable assets: the people doing the work.

CELEBRATING WINS

Progress deserves more than quiet acknowledgment. When organizations take time to recognize what's going well, they reinforce alignment, energize teams, and build a culture rooted in purpose and momentum. Celebration is not a distraction from performance—it is part of it.

The pursuit of mission-aligned excellence can be intense. Strategic goals are ambitious, and the work is often complex and relentless. Without intentional pauses to mark progress, even the most dedicated teams risk losing sight of how much they've achieved. A win—no matter the size—signals that the plan is working. It offers proof that alignment, discipline, and effort are producing real results.

Celebration can take many forms.

- A handwritten thank-you note from a leader.
- Recognition during a staff meeting.
- A visual tracker in the office marking milestones.
- Quarterly appreciation events.
- "Win of the week" emails.
- A traveling trophy.

What matters most is that the recognition is genuine and consistent—it must feel earned, not performative.

Strategic performance is a long game. Acknowledging success along the way sustains energy and keeps morale high—especially when teams are adapting to new systems or tackling complex internal challenges. It also deepens commitment by reinforcing the connection between daily actions and organizational outcomes. When people see that their work moves the mission forward, they show up differently. They take more ownership. They bring more heart.

Celebration also clarifies expectations. It defines what success looks like in real terms—not just in numbers, but in the behaviors and decisions that drive those outcomes. When staff see what is praised and elevated, they understand what to emulate. This builds momentum not only for the current plan, but for a lasting performance culture.

In Mission Aligned Data Driven organizations, wins aren't saved for the finish line. They are built into the journey—recognized, shared, and celebrated as proof that the strategy is not only alive, but thriving.

FINAL THOUGHTS

Performance is not a phase you pass through—it's a standard you live by. It's where mission meets motion, where plans are tested, and where real impact is created. The strategies crafted with care during the planning process only come to life when organizations remain focused, disciplined, and responsive throughout implementation.

This chapter has explored how to maintain that momentum—by staying aligned with strategic priorities, creating feedback loops that foster collaboration and learning, tracking meaningful data, making timely adjustments, protecting the well-being of staff, and recognizing the progress being made. But none of it holds without leadership. Performance is sustained not by systems alone, but by leaders who are present, principled, and persistent.

As your organization moves deeper into implementation, the commitment to performance must remain front and center. Keep the strategy visible, keep the data flowing, keep the people cared for, and above all, keep moving—when plans are lived with intention, missions come to life.

And as the work continues, don't just look at what's been done—look at what it's teaching you. Performance opens the door to insight. In the next chapter, we'll explore how to investigate results with purpose, ask better questions, and turn activity into understanding.

PERFORMANCE

REFLECTION

Use these questions to assess how well your organization is performing in alignment with its strategic goals.

- **Assess**: *Are current programs, practices, and decisions consistently guided by the strategic plan—and supported with adequate data and resources?*

- **Reflect**: *Where might the organization be losing focus, missing feedback, or failing to act on what performance data is revealing?*

- **Act**: *Write down one process in your organization you will commit to strengthening this year.*

CHAPTER 9
INSPECTION

FROM INFORMATION TO INSIGHT

IInspection is the phase in the INSPIRE framework where strategy meets scrutiny. It is the moment when organizations pause—not to admire results, but to examine them; not to celebrate the numbers, but to question what they mean.

This is the most overlooked part of the cycle. Data is collected. Boxes are checked. Dashboards are updated. And then—nothing. The opportunity to learn, grow, and improve quietly slips by because no one slowed down long enough to ask: *What is the data trying to tell us?*

Inspection is not about defending results or proving success. It's about discovering truth. *Who did we help? How were they helped? What changed? What didn't—and why?* This isn't about compliance. It's about clarity. It's about building a culture where data is not just a requirement—it's a resource. A resource for strategy, for equity, for operational alignment, and for mission-driven refinement.

When done well, inspection becomes a habit. Not a quarterly task or an annual ritual, but a regular practice. A way of thinking that infuses every meeting, every discussion, and every strategic decision with curiosity, precision, and purpose.

In this chapter, we'll explore how to use inspection to unlock insight. We'll discuss how to evaluate data quality, introduce key types of analysis, and show how even the most basic performance metrics can yield powerful discoveries. Most importantly, we'll show how analysis doesn't require advanced degrees or expensive tools—it simply requires the willingness to ask a good question and the discipline to follow the answer where it leads.

WHY INSPECTION MATTERS

If performance is the engine that drives change, then evaluation is the compass that tells you whether you're going in the right direction. Without it, organizations may be moving—but they have no way of knowing whether their momentum is meaningful or just motion.

Evaluating data allows leaders to move beyond assumptions and anecdotes. It reveals patterns that aren't visible on the surface—showing who is being served, how well they're progressing, and what kinds of interventions are making the most difference. When organizations stop to examine their results with honest curiosity, they begin to uncover the subtle dynamics that shape success: the gaps in service, the disparities in access, the levers that actually drive transformation.

Evaluation also builds trust. When board members, funders, and partners see that an organization not only tracks outcomes but analyzes them, it signals integrity and intentionality. It shows that leadership is not just committed to action, but to improvement. That they don't just want to do the work—they want to do it well.

And internally, a commitment to evaluation fosters a culture of learning. Teams begin to ask better questions. Conversations shift from blame to inquiry. Staff become more engaged because they can see how their efforts connect to results—and how those results can be refined over time.

Done well, evaluation doesn't just show where an organization has been—it helps chart where it's going. It links activity to impact. It strengthens decision-making. And it lays the foundation for every smart, strategic next step.

THE IMPORTANCE OF DATA QUALITY

Before any inspection can begin, the most important question is not *what does the data say?*—it's *can the data be trusted?* Insight depends on integrity. Even the most well-designed analysis is meaningless if the information feeding it is flawed. In fact, bad data doesn't just obscure the truth—it can lead organizations to make confident decisions that are completely wrong.

Data quality is not a technology issue—it's a culture issue. It requires organizations to treat information with the same seriousness as service. If a case manager fails to provide a client with food or housing, that would be cause for concern. The same standard must apply to incomplete records, incorrect reporting, or missing outcome documentation. The consequences may be less visible, but they are no less real.

High-quality data is complete, accurate, consistent, and timely. Yet too often, agencies overlook these basics in the rush to meet reporting deadlines or juggle competing tasks. Fields get skipped. Outcomes are assumed. Services are entered late or not at all. What's left behind is not a reflection of the organization's work—it's only a shadow.

Every agency should be able to answer: *What percentage of our records are complete? How much of our outcome data is verified? Where are the gaps?* A completion rate of 90–95% is a realistic benchmark in many systems, though the ideal is always to improve from wherever you are. But before improvement is possible, transparency is required.

The goal is not to blame—but to build better systems. That starts with clarity. *What exactly needs to be tracked? Who is responsible? How often is it reviewed?* Strong organizations document not only their services, but the expectations around documentation itself. They train staff on why accuracy matters, not just how to enter data. And they create a culture where information is valued—because they know that when data falls apart, decisions follow.

If performance is about staying on course, then data quality is the map. Without it, you may still be moving—but you'll never be sure where you'll end up.

TYPES OF ANALYSIS

Once data quality is confirmed, the next step is understanding how to make sense of it. This is where analysis begins—not with complex math, but with simple categorization. Different types of analysis answer different kinds of questions. And knowing which type to use is the first step toward using data with purpose.

This section introduces some of the most common analytical approaches used in mission-driven organizations. You don't need to be an analyst to apply them, but understanding their purpose gives you a better chance of using your data with intention—and asking the right questions at the right time.

Descriptive Analysis

Descriptive analysis is the foundation of most evaluation efforts. It provides a structured summary of what occurred during a program or service period, offering clarity about the volume, characteristics, and distribution of activity.

This method focuses on organizing data into digestible formats —totals, percentages, averages, and basic breakdowns. Whether it's the number of individuals served, the demographics of participants, the types of services delivered, or the duration of engagement, descriptive analysis helps translate raw information into usable facts.

Its strength lies in its simplicity. Rather than interpreting or explaining trends, it presents a neutral account of what took place. In doing so, it helps establish a shared understanding across the organization and ensures that everyone is looking at the same baseline information.

Descriptive analysis also serves as a checkpoint for data quality. If standard descriptive reports—such as total services delivered or client demographics—cannot be reliably generated, it may signal issues in data collection or entry. Gaps at this level often point to broader weaknesses in the data infrastructure.

While it doesn't offer insight into causes or consequences, descriptive analysis is essential. It lays the groundwork for all other types of analysis and ensures that interpretation begins with an accurate, well-defined picture of program activity. It provides a starting point for deeper inquiry and helps stakeholders understand the scale and reach of a program.

It also allows you to validate that the right data is being collected —if you can't run a descriptive report on your program's key demographics, outputs, and outcomes, there's a gap in your system.

Comparative Analysis

Comparative analysis builds on the foundation of descriptive data by introducing contrast. It examines how key metrics differ across time periods, populations, locations, or program types—revealing variation that may not be visible in isolated numbers.

This type of analysis helps contextualize results. For example, a completion rate of 65% might seem strong or weak on its own, but when compared to a previous year's 80% or to another program's 50%, its meaning becomes clearer. Comparison adds perspective, helping organizations understand whether performance is consistent, improving, declining, or diverging across areas.

Comparative analysis can be especially helpful in identifying disparities. It highlights where certain populations may experience different outcomes, or where certain services may yield stronger results. It can also uncover differences in cost, efficiency, or reach—providing insight into where programs are performing equitably and where they are not.

Importantly, this form of analysis relies on consistency in how data is collected and categorized. If metrics are defined differently across groups or timeframes, comparisons may become misleading. Maintaining standard definitions and reporting practices ensures that comparisons are valid and useful.

While comparative analysis doesn't explain the reasons behind the differences, it flags the areas where further inquiry is needed. It shows where variation exists—and invites organizations to explore what that variation means.

Trend Analysis

Trend analysis examines how key data points shift over time. Rather than offering a static snapshot, it reveals patterns—highlighting whether something is increasing, decreasing, or remaining stable across multiple time periods.

This approach is especially helpful for identifying sustained changes in performance. When data is organized into consistent intervals—such as months, quarters, or years—it becomes possible to observe movement. Whether a program is expanding its reach, improving its outcomes, or experiencing decline, trend analysis makes those shifts visible.

The value of this method lies in its ability to provide context. A single year's data may seem strong or weak in isolation, but when compared across several cycles, a clearer picture emerges. Positive trends can confirm that a strategy is working, while negative trends can signal the need for intervention.

Trend analysis is also foundational to forecasting and planning. By understanding how indicators have changed historically, organizations are better equipped to anticipate what may come next and adjust their efforts accordingly. While not predictive in nature, it offers a directional view that helps teams prepare with more confidence.

As with any analysis, care must be taken to ensure accuracy and consistency in how the data is collected over time. Missing values or irregular reporting can cloud interpretation. But when applied well, trend analysis transforms scattered results into an organized story of progress.

Predictive Analysis

Predictive analysis is a forward-looking approach that uses existing data to anticipate future outcomes. Rather than focusing on what has already occurred, it identifies patterns and trends that may help forecast what's likely to happen next.

This type of analysis doesn't guarantee future results, but it can help organizations make more informed decisions about where to focus efforts or allocate resources. For example, if historical data shows that participants who complete three or more financial coaching sessions are more likely to achieve budgeting success, predictive analysis may suggest prioritizing early-session engagement to increase future success rates.

In mission-driven organizations, predictive tools can range from simple trend extrapolations to more advanced models built using statistical software. The sophistication of the method often depends on the volume and quality of available data. But even basic pattern recognition can be powerful—especially when it empowers agencies to anticipate needs and act with foresight, rather than responding under pressure.

Predictive analysis should be used carefully. It can reveal likelihoods, not certainties. Results should be interpreted alongside organizational knowledge, environmental context, and the unique needs of clients and communities. It's not about making rigid assumptions—it's about using available information to prepare smarter and lead with greater intention.

Bringing It Together

Organizations do not need to master every analytical method at once. Even consistent use of basic descriptive and comparative analysis can drive meaningful improvement. What matters most is beginning—with curiosity, with discipline, and with the commitment to use data not just to report activity, but to drive learning and impact.

MAKING ANALYSIS SIMPLE

Analytics often sounds intimidating—like a skill reserved for statisticians, data scientists, or consultants with complex software. But at its core, analytics is something far more accessible. It's the art of asking good questions—and being curious enough to follow where the answers lead.

In a Mission Aligned Data Driven organization, analysis isn't a separate task for specialists. It's part of the daily rhythm of decision-making, reflection, and learning. Analytics is simply a structured way of thinking: *What happened? Why did it happen? What does it mean for the future?*

It all starts with curiosity. We ask: *How many people did we serve? Who were they? What changed as a result? Where did we succeed? Where did we fall short? And where must we grow?* Each question leads naturally to the next. Analysis isn't a checklist—it's a conversation. One that grows deeper and more meaningful the longer you engage with it.

Analysis isn't a checklist - it's a conversation.

But meaningful inquiry depends on a solid foundation. If your data is incomplete, fragmented, or locked in systems that don't connect, even the most basic questions may go unanswered—or worse, may lead you astray. Analysis doesn't just require curiosity. It requires infrastructure. You must have the right systems in place to ensure your answers are trustworthy.

In the sections that follow, we'll walk through a series of key questions every mission-driven organization should ask when examining performance. These questions are adapted from the Seven Key Questions first introduced by Reginald Carter in *The Accountable Agency*[1], integrated into the *Introduction to ROMA* by Barbara Mooney and Fred Richmond[2], and expanded to reflect the deeper insights that today's leaders need.

This isn't about complexity—it's about clarity. You don't need to be a data expert to use data well. You just need a system that encourages questions, respects evidence, and stays grounded in the mission. When that happens, analysis becomes not just doable—but indispensable.

How many people did we assist?

This is the most fundamental question in any analysis—and, surprisingly, still one of the most difficult for many organizations to answer with confidence. It's not just about tracking volume—it's about clarity. *How many individual, unduplicated people did the organization actually help?*

In many cases, agencies report the total number of services delivered, not the total number of unique individuals. If one person receives five services, they may be counted five times—unless the system is designed to track unduplicated customers. Without an unduplicated count, nearly every other analysis becomes compromised.

And the issue goes deeper when different programs use different software platforms. If those systems don't "talk" to each other—either through a shared database or a data bridge like an API (Application Programming Interface)—there's no way to know if the same individual is included in multiple places. You may be serving fewer people than you think.

INSPECTION

A true unduplicated count is the foundation for understanding reach. It is essential both at the strategy level (*how many people did this program assist?*) and at the organization-wide level (*how many total people did we serve across all programs?*). Without a true understanding of who is being served—and how many times—it's impossible to assess whether resources are equitably distributed or if strategic goals are being met across programs. Without that clarity, reliable analysis, comparison, and planning remain out of reach. This is the baseline—and it matters more than most people realize.

Who did we assist?

Once we know how many people we served, the next question is: *Who were they?*

Understanding who your customers are is also foundational for conducting other types of analysis. It's not just about counting individuals—it's about understanding the characteristics of those you served, the distinct groups they represent, and the patterns that emerge across different segments of your client base.

This is where demographic and characteristic data becomes essential. Information such as age, gender, race, ethnicity, income level, education, disability status, employment status, and household composition provides the foundation for deeper insight. These data points give critical context to service delivery and allow agencies to assess whether outcomes vary across different populations—and whether equity goals are being met.

This question is also about alignment. During the Navigation phase of the *INSPIRE* framework, your community assessment identified which populations face the greatest levels of need. This is the moment to compare those findings with your actual client data. *Are the individuals being served reflective of the populations your agency set out to reach? Are there groups* present in your community's need profile that are noticeably absent in your client records?

If so, it's time to ask deeper questions: *Which populations are underrepresented in our services? Why are they not accessing support? Are there geographic, cultural, linguistic, technological, or procedural barriers in place?* These are critical insights that emerge simply from examining demographics—and they can shape outreach strategies, refine service models, and ultimately drive more inclusive impact.

When paired with an unduplicated count, demographic data becomes one of the most powerful tools an agency has—not just for reporting who was served, but for driving smarter decisions. It helps leaders allocate resources, design more responsive programs, and ensure equity is not just an aspiration, but an outcome. Before any deeper analysis can begin, we must first be confident in who we reached—and just as importantly, who we didn't.

What challenges were they facing?

Understanding who we served is only part of the story. To truly align services with the mission, we must also ask: *What challenges were they facing—and what kinds of support would help them move forward?*

Need identification should be central to every intake process—not just a box to check or a way to determine program eligibility, but a moment of discovery. A well-designed intake experience helps uncover the full range of barriers someone may be navigating, whether they know how to name them or not. It captures not just what customers ask for, but also what they may need to thrive.

The strongest systems approach this proactively. They use structured assessment tools, logic-based prompts, and well-trained staff to surface issues like under-employment, a lack of transportation, mental health concerns, or inadequate digital access—challenges that often go unspoken.

This approach also plays a critical role in equity. Some needs may only be revealed when someone knows the right question to ask—or is invited into a conversation that sees them as a whole person, not just a program applicant. By embedding discovery into intake, agencies prevent people from being excluded from help they didn't know to request.

And the implications go far beyond individual service. When data on customer needs is collected consistently across the agency, it becomes a strategic asset. It can guide resource development, shape partnerships, and highlight emerging issues across populations or geographies. It becomes the first chapter in a data-informed performance cycle.

Ultimately, identifying needs isn't about gathering information for its own sake. It's about setting the stage for alignment. It provides the foundation for responsive service delivery, informed evaluation, and long-term impact. What happens at intake defines the priorities, possibilities, and pitfalls that shape a program's success from start to finish.

What services did we provide?

Knowing what services your agency delivered may seem obvious—but when it comes to performance analysis, this question goes deeper than a list of activities. It's about understanding the full scope, scale, and purpose of what was offered—and how it connects to the outcomes you hoped to achieve.

To begin, it's important to define services clearly. Some services are easy to track—like providing a utility payment, distributing food, or conducting a workshop. Others are more complex—such as case management or coaching—and may involve multiple interactions over time. Ambiguity in service definitions often leads to inconsistent reporting, making it difficult to compare performance across teams, programs, or sites.

That's why this question is not just what you delivered, but also how and how often. *Were services one-time or ongoing? How many instances of each service were delivered? Were they delivered directly by your agency or through partners? Were customers receiving multiple services simultaneously—or a single, focused intervention?*

Just as importantly, agencies must assess whether the right services were provided to the right people. If clearly identified needs are not met with corresponding services—or are addressed inconsistently—it raises a red flag. This gap may indicate a disconnect between intake, planning, and service delivery, or reveal resource limitations that require strategic attention. If a program is designed to improve financial stability, which specific services within it are responsible for that result? If those services are missing or inconsistently delivered, it signals a breakdown between planning and execution.

These connections are vital, because they shape both evaluation and improvement. Without them, it's difficult to know what's working, what's duplicative, and what needs to be adjusted. Over time, this question also supports analysis of service intensity (*how much support did someone receive?*) and service equity (*are certain groups receiving fewer services than others?*).

Finally, this question must be answered in tandem with the previous two. Knowing who you served, and what you provided to them, allows you to begin linking inputs to outcomes. That's the heart of data-informed improvement—not just documenting activity but understanding its role in creating change.

What changed as a result of our work?

This is the heart of performance analysis. After delivering services and engaging with customers—what actually changed in their lives?

Understanding outcomes requires more than documenting services delivered. It means measuring whether the intended results occurred—and for whom. *Did customers secure employment? Improve their credit? Obtain stable housing? Achieve a personal or family goal?* These are the kinds of changes that reflect mission impact—and they must be tracked with purpose and consistency.

A strong outcome system begins with clarity. As introduced in the Strategy chapter, each program should be anchored by a single primary outcome—clearly defined, measurable, and time-bound. For example, if your program aims to reduce homelessness, then sustained housing stability—tracked over time—is your outcome. Supporting KPIs can monitor incremental progress, but the primary outcome should always define ultimate success. Clarity at this level ensures that results are measurable, verifiable, and aligned with the organization's strategic intent.

In many cases, this includes the use of standardized outcome scales. These tools are particularly effective for tracking incremental improvement, capturing subtle progress that occurs along the way to full resolution. Rather than relying solely on binary measures (e.g., employed or unemployed, housed or homeless), outcome scales allow agencies to recognize and value each step forward. Some performance systems—like the Easytrak software developed by SmartQuest Technology*—even integrate auto-

---

* Easytrak is a web-based performance system used by many nonprofits to track unduplicated counts, outcomes, and incremental progress across programs. It includes integrated outcome scaling, self-sufficiency tracking, and program-specific reporting tools. Contact info@smartquest.net for more information.

mated scaling features directly into the workflow, making it easier to document and visualize progress over time.

This question also allows you to distinguish between activity and effectiveness. A high volume of services means little if no meaningful outcomes follow. However, even a small intervention can have big results if it's well-targeted.

Tracking outcomes also enables more complex analysis over time. *Are results improving or declining? Do certain services lead to stronger results than others? Are outcomes consistent across populations—or are there disparities by race, age, or geography?* These are the kinds of insights that elevate organizational learning and lead to smarter strategy.

In addition to measuring outcomes individually, organizations should also explore how they influence each other. Improvements in one area often create ripple effects in another. Recognizing these interdependencies helps agencies align strategies more effectively, amplify total impact, and adapt services to the interconnected nature of real-world challenges.

Finally, don't just measure outcomes—listen to them. Behind every data point is a person. Investigate both the numbers and the stories. Celebrate what's working. Understand what isn't. And use what you learn to evolve.

Did they receive what they needed?

Achieving outcomes is essential—but so is understanding whether those outcomes addressed the right problems. This question moves beyond success rates to examine alignment: *Did the services provided meaningfully respond to the needs identified?*

It begins with the individual. *Were the barriers reported during intake or assessment directly addressed through the supports received? Were the services tailored to match those needs, or were there gaps between what was offered and what was required?*

These gaps matter. A customer may secure employment, but without childcare support, their long-term stability remains at risk. A household may receive energy assistance, but remain in unsafe housing. These mismatches may not show up in standard outcome reports—but they represent critical threats to lasting progress.

Unmet needs—especially when tracked over time and by population—can also reveal larger equity and access concerns. *Are certain groups more likely to experience service gaps? Are particular needs going unaddressed due to eligibility restrictions, resource shortages, or procedural design?* Recognizing these trends allows agencies to identify patterns of exclusion and respond with intentional change.

Also, unmet needs may represent the missing components that prevent full achievement of the agency's mission. Whether services are delivered directly or through partners, alignment remains the agency's responsibility. These gaps are not failures —they are signals, pointing to where the system must evolve.

This question ultimately challenges organizations to look beyond activity and even beyond outcomes. It asks whether the right supports were delivered, to the right people, at the right time. In doing so, it reinforces a core principle: Mission impact is not measured solely by how many people were served or what was achieved—but by how well those achievements aligned with real human need. And that alignment begins with how well needs were understood at intake—and ends with whether those needs were addressed in practice.

Were the customers satisfied?

Meeting needs and achieving outcomes are critical—but they are only part of the story. An equally important question is: *Were the customers satisfied with their experience?*

Customer satisfaction is often overlooked in traditional performance measurement, yet it offers powerful insight into service quality, accessibility, and respect for the people being served. Even when outcomes are achieved, a poor experience can erode trust, discourage future engagement, and weaken the agency's reputation in the community.

Satisfaction is not just about whether customers "liked" the service—it's about whether they felt heard, respected, supported, and empowered. It reflects how easy or difficult it was to access services, how clearly processes were explained, and whether they felt the organization genuinely cared about their success.

Gathering satisfaction data doesn't have to be complicated. Simple surveys, interviews, or feedback forms—administered at logical points in the service process—can provide valuable information. Key questions might include:

- *How easy was it to access services?*

- *Did staff treat you with respect and dignity?*

- *Did the services meet your expectations?*

- *What could we do to improve?*

Analyzing satisfaction data alongside outcome data offers a more comprehensive picture. For example, high outcome achievement but low satisfaction scores might suggest that results are being delivered at the expense of customer experience. Conversely, high satisfaction with low outcomes may indicate that customers appreciate the effort but are not receiving effective help.

In a Mission Aligned Data Driven organization, customer satisfaction is not an afterthought—it's an essential measure of how well the agency is living out its values. Listening to customer voices strengthens relationships, surfaces operational improvements, and reinforces a culture of respect, learning, and accountability.

What did it cost?

Every service, outcome, and engagement comes with a price—and understanding those costs is essential for both accountability and sustainability. That's why the next core question is: *What did it cost?*

At its most basic, this question refers to the total dollar amount spent to operate a program or run the organization. But meaningful cost analysis goes deeper. It explores not only what was spent, but how resources were allocated—and whether those investments produced meaningful results.

It's not just what you spend - it's what you spend it on, and what you got in return.

This includes direct costs like staffing, supplies, and financial assistance, as well as indirect costs like administrative support, facilities, and technology infrastructure. Clarity and consistency in how costs are tracked and categorized is essential for comparing programs, assessing efficiency, and making informed decisions about scaling or redesigning services.

Understanding cost also supports financial transparency. Board members, funders, and community stakeholders increasingly expect agencies to demonstrate not just how much they spent—but how wisely. When agencies can clearly articulate what it costs to deliver a service or produce a result, they build trust and credibility.

This question sets the stage for deeper exploration in the next section, where we'll examine cost-per-service and cost-per-outcome metrics—and how they can be used to assess organizational efficiency and guide future decisions.

What is the cost per customer served?

Once we know our total costs, the next logical step is to ask: *What did it cost to assist each customer?* This is one of the most straightforward—but powerful—metrics for understanding efficiency.

To calculate this, simply divide total program costs by the number of unduplicated customers served. The result gives you an average cost per customer—an essential benchmark for comparing across programs, years, or geographic areas. But keep in mind, this number is only meaningful if your customer count is accurate. Without an unduplicated count, the entire calculation can be misleading.

Cost per customer is often the first metric that board members, funders, and auditors want to see because it provides a quick understanding of financial stewardship. *Are we reaching enough people for the amount of money spent? Are costs rising or falling over time? Are there programs that cost significantly more—or less—per customer served?*

What did it cost per outcome achieved?

Understanding cost per customer is only part of the equation. To evaluate effectiveness, organizations must also ask: *How much did it cost to achieve each success?* This shifts the focus from volume to value—how well resources translated into meaningful, measurable results.

This figure is calculated by dividing total program costs by the number of successful outcomes. It connects dollars spent directly to impact and offers a clear lens for judging return on investment.

This analysis becomes even more powerful when paired with demographic data. *Do some customer groups require more time, more services, or more funding to achieve the same result?* That's not a failure—it's a reflection of the barriers people face and the support they need. Recognizing these differences allows agencies to allocate resources more equitably and design services that respond to real-world complexity.

Understanding cost per outcome isn't just about cutting expenses, but about knowing what drives them. A higher cost may reflect the intensity of support required to achieve meaningful change. In other cases, variation may highlight inefficiencies or mismatches between services and customer needs. Either way, this metric helps agencies steward resources wisely and invest in strategies that work.

At its best, cost-per-outcome analysis connects financial data to mission impact—making it one of the most practical and revealing tools in any organization's performance toolkit.

Did we meet our targets?

Another important—but often overlooked—questions in data analysis is: *Did we meet our targets?* This is the heart of what's known as performance targeting—the practice of setting specific, measurable goals in advance and then evaluating how actual performance compares to those expectations.

Performance targeting applies across multiple domains: enrollment, outcome achievement, and expenditures. *Did we serve as many people as we planned to? Did participants achieve the outcomes we projected? Did we stay within—or overspend—our budget?* These comparisons allow organizations to move beyond activity tracking and into true accountability.

The value of performance targeting lies not just in tracking success, but in sharpening strategy. If targets are consistently missed, it may indicate deeper issues—gaps in service delivery, misaligned assumptions, or external barriers that weren't anticipated. If targets are always exceeded, it might suggest the original goals were too modest. Either way, these comparisons create

INSPECTION

a feedback loop that strengthens planning and execution over time.

Hitting a target isn't the end - it's the beginning of understanding.

Strong targets are grounded in data. During the Strategy phase, targets for enrollment, success, and financial expenditures are established based on past performance, current capacity, and projected community need. These benchmarks provide the foundation for evaluating success with integrity.

Performance targeting also helps reveal important equity and access issues. For example, if a program meets its overall enrollment goal but falls short among a specific population group, that discrepancy warrants attention. Similarly, if expenditures are on track but outcomes fall behind, it raises questions about efficiency and impact.

Ultimately, performance targeting is about alignment. It helps organizations hold themselves accountable to the plans they created—and to the communities they serve.

From Inquiry to Insight

Taken together, these questions form the foundation of performance analysis. They are not just a checklist. They are a mindset. A Mission Aligned Data Driven organization doesn't wait until the end of the year to ask them. It builds systems that provide answers in real time—and uses the answers to guide action, improve quality, and strengthen outcomes.

DIGGING DEEPER INTO PERFORMANCE ACCURACY

As introduced in the previous section, comparing actual results to projected goals is essential. But it's not enough to simply know whether targets were met. A result that misses the mark by 2% is very different from one that misses by 40%. This distinction matters—not only for accountability, but for learning and decision-making.

Many organizations in the Community Action network use a common benchmark: if performance falls between 80% and 120% of the target, it's considered "on track." This broad range accounts for the natural variability common in human services. But while it's useful, it lacks precision. It doesn't reveal how far off we are—or whether the deviation is cause for concern.

That's where the Mission Aligned Data Driven (MADD) framework takes things a step further. To bring clarity and nuance to the conversation, we use a Modified Sigma Scale. *This scale adapts the core logic of Six Sigma—a methodology rooted in performance accuracy and continuous improvement—and translates it for the nonprofit and public service context.

Why Modify the Scale?

Traditional Six Sigma is designed for high-volume industrial processes aiming for near-zero defects across millions of outputs. But human service programs operate in a very different context

---

* Visit https://sahowellco.com/perfomance-calculator/ to access the MADD Performance Calculator, demonstrating the modified Six Sigma Scale.

—working with smaller sample sizes, dynamic human needs, and real-world constraints. Perfection isn't always realistic, and variability is expected.

For that reason, the Modified Sigma Scale re-centers the 3 Sigma range around the widely accepted performance benchmark of 80–120% performance targeting accuracy, using a standard deviation of 6.67%. This adaptation maintains the spirit of Six Sigma —continuous improvement, data-informed inquiry, and process reliability—while grounding it in the practical realities of mission-driven work.

The Modified Sigma Scale

- **6 Sigma (100%)**
    - Perfect Performance
    - *Exact alignment with no detected deviation*

- **5 Sigma (93.33 - 106.67%)**
    - Optimal Performance
    - *Near-perfect alignment with minor deviation*

- **4 Sigma (86.67 - 113.33%)**
    - Good Performance
    - *Reliable execution with moderate deviation*

- **3 Sigma (80.00 – 120.00%)**
    - Acceptable Performance
    - *Within allowable parameters with notable deviation*

- **2 Sigma (73.33 - 126.67%)**
    - Unacceptable Performance
    - *Outside of allowable parameters with significant deviation*

- **1 Sigma (66.67 - 133.33%)**
    - Critical Deviation
    - *Outside of allowable parameters with extreme deviation*

- **Below 1 Sigma (<66.67% or >133.33%)**
    - Targeting failure
    - *Major breakdown in delivery or planning*

This framework provides a clearer picture—not just whether performance was in range, but where it falls on a scale of stability and reliability. It creates a structured, shared language for interpreting results across programs and teams.

Example:

A program established a performance target for 80 out of 100 customers to secure employment within 12 months. This projection defined the intended benchmark for success.

At the end of the reporting period, 60 participants had successfully achieved the employment outcome.

Performance targeting accuracy is calculated by dividing the actual results by the projected target:

$60 \div 80 = 0.75$, or 75% targeting accuracy.

This figure reflects how closely actual performance aligned with the original plan—not simply the outcome rate, but the precision of forecasting and delivery.

Under the Modified Sigma Scale, a targeting accuracy of 75% equates to a modified sigma level of 2.75, falling short of the typical benchmark of 80–120%, which is designated as 3 Sigma ("Acceptable Performance").

INSPECTION

This does not indicate program failure. However, it does signal the need for deeper inspection into potential contributing factors, such as:

- Whether the original targets were realistic given the customer base and service environment.

- Whether participant barriers or support needs were underestimated.

- Whether sufficient programmatic supports were provided throughout the service period.

- Whether external factors beyond the agency's control impacted outcomes.

The strength of the Sigma approach lies not in assigning blame, but in sharpening inquiry. It creates a structured, data-informed framework that helps organizations move beyond anecdote, fostering reflection, learning, and strategic improvement.

In a Mission Aligned Data Driven organization, Sigma evaluation is not the end of the conversation—it is the beginning. It transforms measurement into momentum, and insight into action.

WHAT THE NUMBERS REVEAL

To bring performance analysis to life, sometimes the most powerful tool is a single example. Stories like this play out in agencies across the country every year. What follows is a simplified—but very real—illustration of how numbers can expose disconnects between intention, execution, and impact.

MISSION ALIGNED.DATA DRIVEN.

	Projected	Actual	Percent
Expenditures	$15,000	$6,000	40%
Customers	200	35	17%
Success	80	3	4%
Client Cost	$75	$171	228%
Success Cost	$187	$2,000	1,070%

A program was funded with $15,000 to serve customers over a one-year period. Based on strategic planning estimates, the agency projected that the funding would support 200 participants at a cost of $75 per person. Of those 200, approximately 80 were expected to achieve the program's primary outcome—yielding a projected success cost of $187 per outcome achieved.

But by year's end, only $6,000 of the allocated funding had been spent. On the surface, this might appear fiscally conservative. However, unspent dollars do not always signal efficiency—especially when outcomes are left on the table. In this case, lower spending meant fewer services were delivered. Only 35 people were served as compared to the 200 that were projected.

To calculate how much of the original service goal was met, divide the actual number served (35) by the projected number (200):

35 ÷ 200 = 0.175, or 17.5% of the target

Now examine cost per customer. Divide the actual dollars spent ($6,000) by the number of people served (35).

$6,000 ÷ 35 = $171 per customer

That's more than double the original projection of $75 per person.

But the greatest concern lies in the program's intended result: outcomes.

Only 3 of the 35 participants achieved the success outcome. Compared to the original goal of 80 successes, that's just:

3 ÷ 80 = 0.0375, or 3.75% of the targeted impact

On the Modified Sigma Scale, that 4% performance accuracy equates to approximately 0.06 —well below the acceptable range.

And cost per successful outcome? Take the $6,000 in expenditures and divide it by the number of actual successes:

$6,000 ÷ 3 = $2,000 per outcome

That is more than ten times the cost that was initially projected.

Let's step back:

40% of the funds were used:
$6,000 as compared to $15,000

17% of the customers were served:
35 as compared to 200

4% of the outcomes were achieved:
3 as compared to 80

If this were a private business, delivering only 4% of the product while using 40% of the budget would prompt immediate scrutiny. In nonprofit and public sector work, however, performance data is not always evaluated with that same rigor. Reports are filed, funding is reconciled—but few pause to ask: *What happened? Why did it happen? And what must change?*

These are not rhetorical questions. They are essential for stewardship, learning, and growth.

Consistently underspending your grant funding can raise red flags with funders, especially when paired with low outcomes. Future allocations may be reduced under the assumption that the agency lacks the capacity to manage and deliver on its funding. At the same time, outcomes that are dramatically below projection demand a strategic response—not excuses, but understanding. *Was $6,000 truly the maximum amount that could be utilized? Were outreach efforts effective? Were staff trained and supported? Were barriers to participation underestimated? Was the definition of success too narrow—or the documentation process incomplete?*

This is where performance inspection becomes critical. If a success isn't recorded, it isn't counted. But if a success is recorded without documentation, it isn't credible. Data integrity matters—not only to funders and auditors, but to the agency's own capacity to lead with confidence.

Ultimately, the role of evaluation is not to assign blame. It is to shine light—on what worked, what didn't, and what must change. Numbers don't need to be perfect. But they do need to be understood.

And if you're not asking what the numbers reveal, you may be reporting on your programs without ever truly managing them.

INSPECTION

In a Mission Aligned Data Driven organization, we don't just report performance—we interpret it, challenge it, and use it to build better futures.

FINAL THOUGHTS

Inspection is where understanding begins. It serves as the bridge between action and insight—between collecting data and truly using it. Without a commitment to inspection, organizations risk mistaking activity for impact and compliance for effectiveness. It is not enough to gather data or report outcomes. Progress demands interpretation, inquiry, and the courage to ask what the numbers are actually saying.

This chapter has walked through what it means to ask the right questions—about customers, needs, services, outcomes, costs, and targets—and to answer them with integrity, curiosity, and clarity. It introduced a modified Sigma framework to help quantify how close performance landed to expectations, and explored how deeper analysis can uncover the real story behind the numbers.

But this work is not just technical—it's cultural. It's about building a shared commitment to truth-seeking, learning, and improvement. In a Mission Aligned Data Driven organization, inspection isn't just an exercise in accountability. It's a habit of leadership.

The data may not be perfect, and the answers may not always be easy—but knowing where you stand is the first step to meaningful progress. Growth begins with awareness. When organizations truly commit to understanding their performance—with honesty and depth—they unlock the power to adapt, improve, and lead with greater purpose.

REFLECTION

Use these questions to assess your organization's capacity for meaningful inspection:

- **Assess:** *Are performance results analyzed consistently—or just reported?*

- **Reflect:** *Which questions are you routinely asking of your data—and which ones are you avoiding? Where might you be overestimating success or overlooking problems?*

- **Act:** *Write down one way you can can start strengthening your data inspection today.*

CHAPTER 10
REPORTING

REFRAMING REPORTING AS STRATEGIC COMMUNICATION

In a Mission Aligned Data Driven (MADD) organization, reporting is more than just submitting a list of activities and achievements to a funder. It is a strategic process designed to tell the story of mission impact—carefully and deliberately—to the audiences that matter most.

Strategic communication is how a MADD organization drives deeper engagement:

- Financial support from funders and donors

- Volunteer participation from community members and stakeholders

- Advocacy from elected officials, partners, and the public

Data alone does not inspire action. People invest their time, money, and voice based on what they understand, what they believe, and what they feel compelled to support. Strategic communication ensures that the organization's true story is told —and told in a way that mobilizes others to act.

To guide this process, the MADD framework draws from the foundational work of Wilbur Schramm, one of the most influential figures in modern communication theory.

WHO WAS WILBUR SCHRAMM?

Wilbur Schramm (1907–1987) is often called the father of communication studies. Originally trained as a journalist and educator, Schramm founded the first academic programs in communication at the University of Iowa, the University of Illinois, and Stanford University. His career marked the birth of communication research as a distinct and vital academic discipline.

In 1954, Schramm introduced what would become one of the most recognized models of communication—the Schramm Model[1].

At the time, most communication models were very mechanical: a sender transmits a message to a receiver. But Schramm's model introduced a critical new element: shared meaning.

Schramm emphasized that communication is not successful simply because a message is sent—it is only successful when a message is received, understood, and interpreted accurately within the receiver's own context or experience.

He also highlighted the importance of feedback, making communication a continuous loop rather than a one-way action. This was revolutionary for the time and shifted communication theory away from rigid information delivery and toward dynamic, audience-centered interaction.

Today, Schramm's model remains one of the most respected frameworks in communication studies. It is cited across disciplines—from business, education, and media to nonprofit leadership and organizational strategy. His insights serve as a constant reminder that communication is not about what we say. It is about what is understood.

In the MADD framework, we simplify Schramm's concepts into a practical set of guiding questions—questions that help organizations strategically design their communication so that their data is not just shared, but believed, remembered, and acted upon.

Before we explore those questions, let's take a closer look at the principles behind Schramm's model—and why they are essential for telling the story of impact.

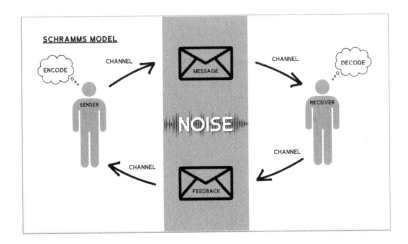

SCHRAMM'S MODEL OF COMMUNICATION

Understanding Schramm's core components helps MADD organizations design communications that do more than inform—they inspire.

The model consists of six fundamental elements:

- **Sender (Encoder):** The person or organization creating the message

- **Message:** The content of what is being shared

- **Medium:** The channel used to send the message (e.g., television, radio, social media)

- **Receiver (Decoder):** The person or group receiving the message

- **Feedback:** The response from the receiver that tells the sender if the message was received and understood

- **Field of Experience:** The shared background, knowledge, or understanding that allows the message to be interpreted correctly

Schramm's critical insight was this: Successful communication depends on shared context.

If the sender and receiver do not have enough overlap in their field of experience, the message may be heard—but not understood.

This insight is especially critical for mission-driven organizations. Many of the audiences we need to engage—funders, policymakers, partners, community members—do not live inside our daily work. They may not fully understand poverty, case management, community action, or social determinants of health. If we fail to bridge the gap between their experience and our mission, even the most accurate data can fail to persuade.

And here's the deeper truth:

Your organization is always telling a story—whether intentionally or not.

Every report, social media post, conversation, and media article shapes how people perceive your work. The only question is: *Are you shaping the story, or letting it shape itself?* In today's politically divided environment, this responsibility is even greater. Social programs and nonprofit efforts are often misunderstood, mischaracterized, or even demonized by those outside the field. If organizations do not clearly and consistently tell their own story—anchored in data, mission, and community impact—they risk having that story told for them in ways that are incomplete, inaccurate, or harmful.

In a MADD organization, strategic communication becomes part of performance itself. It is how you ensure the story of impact is told clearly, intentionally, and persuasively turning numbers into momentum, and data into community action.

MOVING FROM THEORY TO ACTION

With these insights in mind, the MADD framework translates Schramm's principles into action. It simplifies key communication concepts into a practical set of guiding questions—designed not as a compliance checklist, but as a strategic tool. These questions help ensure that every report, social media post, town hall presentation, and grant narrative is purposeful, audience-centered, and mission-aligned.

MISSION ALIGNED.DATA DRIVEN.

In the following sections, we will explore five essential questions that drive effective communication:

- ***Who*** *needs to know about the organization and its work in order to promote fulfillment of the mission?*

- ***Why*** *do we need to communicate with them?*

- ***What*** *do they need to know in order to take the desired action?*

- ***How*** *will we reach them most effectively?*

- ***When*** *and how often should we engage them?*

Each question plays a vital role in translating data into momentum and ensuring that the story of impact is not only shared—but heard, understood, and believed.

Later, we will also explore two additional communication principles:

- How to minimize **noise** that can distort or block your message.

- How to create **feedback loops** that strengthen understanding and deepen relationships over time.

Together, these tools will help you ensure that the story being told about your organization is the story you intend—not the one someone misinterprets from a pie chart or a statistic alone.

Who Needs to Know?

One of the most common mistakes in strategic communication is assuming a single message can serve every audience. It cannot. Even well-crafted statements are filtered through each person's experiences, values, and assumptions. What resonates with one group may confuse—or even alienate—another. Effective communication isn't just about sending information. It's about knowing exactly who needs to receive it—and how they're likely to interpret it.

In a MADD organization, communication begins by asking: *Who needs to know about the organization and its work in order to promote fulfillment of the mission?*

To prioritize communication effectively, it helps to classify your audiences into three strategic groups.

1. Impact
Groups that are directly affected by the organization's mission.

2. Influence
Groups that shape or control the organization's ability to achieve the mission.

3. Investment
Groups who have entrusted us with time, money, or reputation.

Once you understand the role each audience plays, you can tailor your communication with greater precision.

- **Policymakers and elected officials** who influence funding, legislation, and public perception.

- **Businesses**, from small local enterprises to major corporations, who shape economic ecosystems.

- **Community organizations** such as schools, faith-based groups, and fellow nonprofits who can serve as allies, amplifiers, or partners.

- **Community members**, including both those served directly and the broader public whose perceptions shape reputation, advocacy, and investment.

Yet even within these categories, meaningful differences exist. A Democratic and Republican legislator may share concern for poverty, but their views on solutions and success will differ. A small business owner and a corporate executive may both value economic development—but for different reasons. Strategic communication honors these nuances by tailoring messages that reflect each audience's perspective.

Effective communication begins by acknowledging these differences—and designing strategies that respect them.

This requires understanding two key building blocks:

- Demographics: The tangible characteristics of an audience (age, race, gender, geography, language, education, occupation, family structure).

- Psychographics: The intangible drivers (values, beliefs, motivations, attitudes, lifestyle preferences, media habits).

Demographics help you identify who the audience is. Psychographics help you understand how to speak to them in a way that matters. But understanding these traits is only useful if you apply them intentionally.

To make this understanding actionable, organizations often develop personas—fictional but evidence-based profiles that represent typical members of a key audience segment. Personas help communicators move beyond generic messaging by capturing both demographic traits (such as age, education, or occupation) and psychographic factors (like values, motivations, and communication preferences).

While a persona does not represent every individual within a population, it reflects the shared characteristics of a core group. The goal is not to stereotype, but to clarify and focus communication strategies around the common drivers that influence how people receive and respond to messages.

The concept of personas originated in the field of user-centered design. In the early 1980s, software designer Alan Cooper developed the first persona, "Kathy," to guide the design of a project management program.[2] He formalized this approach in his 1998 book, *The Inmates Are Running the Asylum*, introducing personas as a practical tool for creating user-focused designs.[3]

Since then, personas have been widely adopted across various fields, including marketing, public health, and organizational strategy, to shape more effective outreach and engagement. In the MADD framework, personas provide a practical bridge between data and communication—ensuring messages are not only accurate but also compelling and resonant for the people who matter most.

> **Understanding your audience isn't just a communication tactic—it's a form of respect. Personas help us show that respect with every message we send.**

Personas may be fictional, but they are grounded in truth. When crafted thoughtfully, they reflect the hopes, challenges, and values of real people. The following example brings these ideas to life—demonstrating how demographic and psychographic insights can shape a communication strategy that feels personal, relevant, and mission-aligned.

Example Persona:

Name: Marcus Green
Role: Small Business Owner

Demographics:
African American male, age 52, married with two adult children. High school graduate with some vocational coursework. Lifelong resident of a mid-sized Southern town. Owns both a home and a separate property for his landscaping business, which employs 10 local workers.

Psychographics:
Values local solutions, personal responsibility, and second chances. Skeptical of large-scale programs unless they demonstrate real-world results. Supports workforce development tied directly to employment, and services that help families stay stable. Regular Facebook user, listens to local talk radio, and closely follows how public funds are used. Known for his community involvement and pragmatic, common-sense approach.

Motivations:
Wants a safer, stronger community with more opportunity for local youth. Supports initiatives that grow small business, reduce crime, and develop a skilled local workforce.

When communicating to someone like Marcus, a report emphasizing job training results, small business impact, and economic self-sufficiency—delivered through trusted local channels—would resonate far more than one framed in abstract policy language or national narratives.

Building personas isn't about stereotyping audiences. It's about honoring their lived realities—and respecting them enough to craft communication that speaks to their values and priorities.

Why Do We Need to Communicate With Them?

Identifying your audience is only the first step. The next is clarifying why you need to reach them.

This isn't a theoretical exercise—it defines the purpose behind every communication effort. It sharpens the message, clarifies the outcome, and centers the ask: *What role do we want this audience to play in advancing the mission?*

Every communication should move beyond awareness toward meaningful action. Whether the goal is to secure funding, build partnerships, influence policy, or increase participation, the message must be crafted with that end in mind.

The "why" will vary by audience and persona. Understanding each group's motivations, concerns, values, and potential contributions is essential for designing messages that resonate—and drive engagement.

For example:

- When communicating with a politician, the "why" might be to secure political support—leading to actions like sponsoring legislation or approving funding.

- When engaging a business owner, the "why" might be to encourage financial sponsorship or collaboration—resulting in meetings, donations, or co-branded efforts.

- When collaborating with local organizations, the "why" might be to initiate partnerships—leading to shared services or joint advocacy.

- When reaching out to community members, the "why" might range from promoting program participation to mobilizing volunteers and advocates.

Without a clear "why," messaging risks becoming generic, unfocused, or forgettable.

Ultimately, we communicate not just to share information, but to align mission and motivation—and to mobilize others toward the future we are working to build.

What Do They Need to Know?

Once you know who you're communicating with and why, the next question is: *What do they need to know that would encourage them to act?*

This is where many well-intentioned organizations stumble. They flood audiences with data, success stories, and achievements—without filtering the message through the lens of audience priorities. Information without relevance is noise. Information with relevance becomes fuel for action.

The same core data can (and should) be framed differently depending on the audience. What you choose to emphasize—and how you tell the story—should reflect what matters most to the people you're trying to engage.

For example:

- Funders may want proof of outcomes, scalability, and return on investment.

- Elected officials may want evidence of public support, political alignment, and constituent benefit.

- Community members may want personal stories, neighborhood relevance, and a sense of shared success.

- Potential partners want to see strategic alignment, complementary goals, and clear pathways to collaboration.

In communication strategy, this is often described by the WIIFM principle: "What's In It For Me?" Every effective message answers that question for the audience—clearly and quickly.

Even within broad audience categories, meaningful differences exist. A message that resonates with one group may fall flat—or even backfire—with another. For instance, a Democratic legislator may champion your anti-poverty initiative because it aligns with values like family well-being, child welfare, and equity. A Republican legislator may support the same initiative because it reduces long-term public expenditures, increases self-sufficiency, and strengthens the local economy. Both versions are accurate. Both are rooted in real data. But each frames the story in a way that aligns with the listener's values.

This isn't about spin or manipulation. Strategic communication is about building a bridge between your mission and your audience's priorities. It doesn't distort the truth—it clarifies the relevance. When you tailor your message to help others see how your work connects to what they already care about, you create space for shared understanding, deeper alignment, and meaningful action.

How Will We Reach Them?

Once we know who we need to reach, why we need to reach them, and what they need to know, the next essential question is: *How do we deliver that message so that it actually gets through?*

The right message delivered through the wrong channel is still a missed opportunity. Choosing the right communication channel is not a technical decision—it is a strategic one. It directly influences how a message is received, whether it builds trust, and whether it inspires action.

Different audiences consume information through different means. Some rely heavily on social media. Some place more trust in traditional news outlets. Some respond best to direct personal outreach. Others are moved by community events and public forums. To communicate effectively, organizations must meet each audience where they already are—not expect them to find us.

There are many types of communication channels available, including:

- Television and Streaming Platforms

- Radio and Podcasts

- Newspapers and Magazines

- Direct Mail and Print Materials

- Websites, Blogs, and Email Campaigns

- Social Media Platforms

- Public Events, Town Halls, and Community Meetings

- Personal Outreach and Relationship Management

Each channel carries its own strengths—and its own audience behaviors. Even within a category like social media, different platforms attract different populations. For example, Facebook, Instagram, and LinkedIn each appeal to distinct age groups, professional sectors, and cultural demographics.

However, these patterns are not static. Media consumption habits evolve rapidly. The platforms that dominate today may fade tomorrow. New technologies and shifting audience preferences continually reshape the communication landscape.

That is why MADD organizations cannot rely solely on assumptions or past experience.

Effective communication strategies must be rooted in ongoing research, real-time audience feedback, and performance data. Organizations must regularly ask:

- *Where are our audiences actually spending their time now?*

- *Which platforms are gaining or losing trust?*

- *What formats (text, video, audio) are driving the strongest engagement?*

- *How do our different target populations prefer to receive information today—not last year?*

By continually monitoring audience behaviors and adapting outreach methods accordingly, organizations ensure that their strategic communication remains vibrant, relevant, and effective.

Ultimately, the goal is not to master a particular platform, but to master the art of connection.

The channel is simply the bridge. What matters most is that the bridge is built to reach your audience—wherever they are, and however they are ready to listen.

When and How Often Should We Engage Them?

Timing is as critical to communication as the message itself. A brilliant story delivered at the wrong moment, or repeated so often that it fades into background noise, will not achieve its intended impact. In a Mission Aligned Data Driven organization, communication is understood as an ongoing relationship—not a one-time event. How and when you engage with your audiences determines whether you build momentum or lose attention.

Every channel and every audience has its own rhythm. Traditional media, such as television, radio, and newspapers, often respond best to timely, event-driven communication: a major program launch, a new report, or a public advocacy effort tied to legislative sessions or community milestones. Social media, on the other hand, demands more frequent engagement to maintain visibility, but frequency must be purposeful. Posting simply for the sake of staying active can quickly become counterproductive. Without relevance and value, even frequent communication becomes noise.

Email newsletters and direct mail require a different cadence. Regular, scheduled updates—such as quarterly newsletters or annual reports—keep funders, stakeholders, and community members informed without overwhelming them. Personal outreach to key partners, donors, or elected officials must be even more strategic, often aligned to budget planning periods, grant cycles, or moments of political opportunity.

The key is not to chase volume but to build consistency. Organizations that communicate sporadically risk appearing disorganized or disconnected. Those that maintain a steady, thoughtful presence, on the other hand, establish credibility and trust. Audiences come to expect—and respect—the regular cadence, recognizing the organization as one that is active, professional, and mission-driven.

Still, more communication is not always better. Oversaturating an audience with constant updates dilutes the power of each message and can lead to disengagement. Strategic pacing ensures that each communication feels intentional, not intrusive.

Timing should also align with broader movements and moments that matter. Announcing a workforce training success during National Workforce Development Month or highlighting a food security program during Hunger Action Month, ties local stories to national conversations—amplifying visibility and relevance.

Finally, it is important to remember that communication strategy must remain flexible. What works today may shift tomorrow as audience preferences, platform algorithms, and cultural moments evolve. Monitoring response rates, engagement levels, and feedback over time provides vital signals about when to adjust, accelerate, or slow down.

At its core, strategic timing is a form of respect. It recognizes that audiences have limited attention—and that our job is not simply to speak, but to speak at the right moment, in the right way, to those ready to listen and act.

NAVIGATING NOISE

Even the most carefully crafted message can be distorted once it leaves the sender. In communication theory, this distortion is known as noise—anything that interferes with the transmission, reception, or understanding of a message.

In the context of a MADD organization, noise is more than background static. It is a direct threat to impact. It can twist meaning, dilute trust, and compromise mission advancement. It doesn't attack the message directly—it alters how that message is received and understood.

Sometimes noise is obvious and physical: a loud hallway during a presentation, a glitching microphone during a webinar, or a busy web page where key information is buried under cluttered graphics. Other times, it is psychological, cultural, or organizational. A stakeholder's personal stress, biases, or cultural frameworks can interfere with their ability to truly hear and/or trust what you are trying to say.

Often, noise arises not from the environment or the audience, but from the organization itself. Fonts that are too small, jargon-filled language, pixelated logos, unclear charts, dense paragraphs, or poorly printed materials all introduce barriers. Instead of strengthening clarity, they create friction, confusion, or even resistance.

In short: everything matters. The words you choose. The style you adopt. The colors, images, and layouts you use. The timing of delivery. Each of these elements either promotes clarity—or invites noise.

At its core, noise interferes with decoding. This is the critical process by which the receiver interprets a message. When noise overwhelms the signal, the intended meaning is lost. Sometimes it is softened. Sometimes it is twisted. Sometimes it is replaced altogether by assumptions the organization never intended to convey.

In a MADD organization, awareness of noise is not an afterthought.

It is a frontline responsibility.

Every communication effort must be approached with critical questions:

- *Is the environment conducive to clear listening or reading?*

- *Is the message phrased in a way that respects and reflects the audience's field of experience?*

- *Are the visuals, branding, and materials clear, consistent, and professional?*

- *Have potential biases, misunderstandings, and cultural assumptions been considered and addressed?*

Strategic communication is not simply about crafting a compelling message. It is about clearing the path for that message to be received—clearly, fully, and as intended.

Reducing noise demands discipline: simplicity in design, precision in language, intentionality in format, and deep respect for the lived realities of the audiences we seek to engage. It means evaluating not only what we say, but how we say it, and how easy we make it for others to truly hear it.

REPORTING

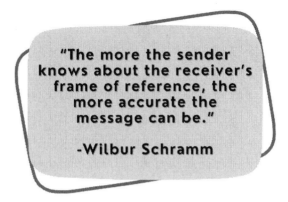

When noise is minimized, messages do not merely arrive. They land. They connect. They move people to act.

BUILDING FEEDBACK LOOPS

In the Schramm Model of communication, feedback is not optional. It's essential. Communication isn't complete until the sender knows whether the message was received, understood, and interpreted as intended. Without feedback, the impact of communication remains uncertain.

In a MADD organization, feedback goes far beyond basic confirmation. It becomes a powerful strategic tool—transforming communication from a one-way broadcast into a two-way dialogue. It strengthens relationships, sharpens messaging, and deepens trust.

This commitment to dialogue aligns with the *Catchball* approach introduced earlier in the book. In traditional Hoshin Kanri, Catchball keeps ideas moving—refined through back-and-forth exchange rather than dictated top-down. In the MADD framework, this same principle is extended outward. We don't just pass ideas between internal teams—we engage stakeholders, funders, elected officials, and community members in that same strategic dialogue.

It's not enough to speak at people. We must speak with them. It's not enough to report results—we must understand how those results are being experienced and perceived on the ground.

Feedback loops are what turn outreach into engagement. When community members offer input—and see it reflected in programs—they become champions. When funders are invited into transparent conversations about outcomes and challenges, they shift from passive check-writers to active allies. When elected officials see programs solving real problems for their constituents, they become advocates rather than bystanders.

But feedback requires more than structure. It requires humility. A willingness to listen, learn, and adjust when feedback reveals blind spots or unmet needs.

When done well, feedback loops don't just improve communication—they transform it. They build trust. They shape strategy. And they elevate everyone involved from passive recipients to active participants in the mission.

In a Mission Aligned Data Driven organization, communication is never a monologue. It is a conversation—one that listens as powerfully as it speaks, and one that turns voices into momentum for change.

FINAL THOUGHTS

Strategic communication is not simply about sharing information. It is about shaping understanding, building trust, and moving people to action—so that your organization can more fully achieve its purpose. In a Mission Aligned Data Driven (MADD) organization, communication is treated not as an afterthought, but as an essential driver of impact.

Throughout this chapter, we have explored how intentional communication—grounded in Schramm's model, strengthened by Hoshin Kanri principles, and focused through the MADD framework—ensures that the organization's true story is heard, believed, and remembered. We have seen that successful communication requires clarity about who needs to know, why they need to know, what they need to know, how they will hear it, and when they are most ready to listen. We have also seen the importance of minimizing noise and establishing feedback loops to foster lasting connection and trust.

At its core, communication is leadership. Every report, post, speech, and conversation is an opportunity to lead—to extend the mission into the world with integrity, precision, and care—and to invite others to become part of it.

When we approach communication with the same rigor we apply to data collection, program design, and service delivery, something powerful happens. Impact is no longer hidden within spreadsheets or buried in annual reports. It is visible. It is compelling. It motivates action. It invites funders, volunteers, policymakers, and community members alike to become part of the mission's next chapter.

Because in the end, the story of an organization is not what it says about itself. It is what others understand, believe, and are moved to support.

MISSION ALIGNED.DATA DRIVEN.

And in a Mission Aligned Data Driven organization, that story is far too important to leave to chance.

REFLECTION

Use these questions to evaluate how effectively your organization is communicating its mission and impact:

- **Assess:** *Are your communications designed with the audience in mind—ensuring that our messages are understood, trusted, and compelling across different groups?*

- **Reflect:** *Where might noise, assumptions, or missed feedback be interfering with how your story is received? Are you inviting meaningful dialogue with the people you serve and depend on?*

- **Act:** *Write down one target population that you will start to develop a communication plan for in the coming week.*[*]

---

[*] A sample communication plan template can be found at https://sahowellco.com/document-library/.

CHAPTER 11
ENRICHMENT

THE JOURNEY HAS NO FINISH LINE

When we began this journey, we asked a simple but powerful question: *What does true excellence look like—and how is it achieved?* Throughout this book, we have explored frameworks, principles, and practices designed to move organizations closer to that ideal. We've built a model for excellence that is grounded in mission, guided by data, strengthened by strategy, and brought to life through communication and action.

But as we reach this final stage—Enrichment—one truth becomes undeniable: excellence is not a destination. It is a discipline. It is not a place that organizations arrive at and then rest. It is a posture they adopt—a way of thinking, acting, and leading that demands continuous refinement. Enrichment is where that discipline is put into practice. It is the phase that sustains progress through a culture of ongoing learning, iteration, and improvement.

In a Mission Aligned Data Driven (MADD) organization, continuous improvement is not an optional phase reserved for "when there's time." It is embedded in the daily rhythm of decisions, service delivery, evaluation, and culture itself.

While every phase of the MADD framework is critical, the ultimate goal is not simply to create better systems. It is to INSPIRE teams to embrace the mindset of continuous improvement. To create a culture where excellence is not enforced but chosen. Where growth is not a response to crisis, but a daily commitment.

Mission-driven organizations cannot afford complacency. Community needs evolve. Economic realities shift. New challenges emerge. What was considered best practice yesterday may be wholly inadequate tomorrow. Excellence belongs to those who are willing to question, learn, and adapt—constantly.

That's the difference between sustaining impact and slipping into irrelevance. Excellence requires discipline. Not just the discipline to do the work—but to question it. To test it. To ask whether our current approach is still the best expression of our mission.

Continuous improvement is not about chasing perfection. It is about honoring the mission enough to ask, over and over again: *How can we do this better?* It requires humility to admit that better is possible. It requires courage to seek it out. And it demands a relentless commitment to learning—not just from success, but from setbacks, mistakes, and missed opportunities.

In a Mission Aligned Data Driven organization, excellence is not measured by the goals that have already been achieved. It is measured by the refusal to stand still.

ENRICHMENT

WHY CONTINUOUS IMPROVEMENT MATTERS

The bottom line is that organizations generally don't fail because they stop caring. They fail because they stop improving.

In every field—technology, healthcare, transportation, education, manufacturing—leaders have embraced the simple but powerful truth that excellence cannot stand still. Products that once led the market become obsolete. Services that once dazzled customers fall behind. Companies that ignore innovation are replaced by those who move faster, listen better, and deliver more. The marketplace doesn't pause to reward past success.

The nonprofit world is no different. While we may not sell products, we do deliver outcomes. Our work is measured not in profit margins but in lives changed, families stabilized, systems improved, and futures restored. And if we do not evolve—if we do not sharpen our methods, question our assumptions, and refine our models—then someone else will. Or worse, the needs we address will go unmet, and communities will suffer.

That's why continuous improvement is not just an operational preference—it's an organizational imperative. It is the single thread that runs through nearly every respected framework used in high-performing environments. In Lean, it's the removal of waste and the pursuit of efficiency. In Six Sigma, it's the reduction of variation and elevation of quality. In Scrum, it's the sprint-review-retrospective cycle that rewards adaptability. In Hoshin Kanri, it's the structured alignment of priorities across teams, paired with reflective dialogue to keep strategy moving. In Project Management Professional (PMP) practice, it's the focus on iterative learning—reviewing what worked and what didn't. In Data-Driven Decision-Making (DDDM), it's the discipline of using feedback to guide smarter action.

Even the *Results Oriented Management and Accountability (ROMA)* cycle used in Community Action reflects this core principle—represented by the arrows that continuously drive the process forward.

Across all of these approaches, the message is consistent: relevance is earned through reflection. Excellence is achieved through iteration, and long-term impact is sustained only by those who make learning part of their culture—not just their crisis response.

In organizations without this mindset, the signs of stagnation are easy to spot: outcomes plateau, innovation slows, and strategy becomes reactive. Success is assumed rather than examined. Decisions are made based on precedent, not performance. This is how well-meaning teams become complacent—delivering services without questioning whether those services still deliver results.

But in organizations committed to continuous improvement, the culture looks different. Teams are empowered to ask, *Is this still the best way?* Leaders expect learning, not perfection. Feedback loops are trusted. Staff are encouraged to challenge the process—not to cause disruption, but to create progress. The organization doesn't wait for failure to course-correct; it adapts because growth is part of its DNA.

Continuous improvement matters because excellence is fragile. It can't be stored. It has to be renewed—every day, through disciplined action and intentional learning. It's not a reaction to crisis. It's a commitment to the mission.

CULTURE AS THE ENGINE OF IMPROVEMENT

You can write the best strategy, fund the best programs, and build the most efficient systems—but if your culture doesn't

ENRICHMENT

support continuous improvement, none of it will last.

Culture is the engine that determines the direction and pace of an organization's growth. It shapes how people make decisions, how they respond to feedback, how they interpret data, and how they react when things don't go as planned. It's not defined by what's written in a handbook. It's revealed in what's tolerated, what's rewarded, and what's ignored.

In a culture of continuous improvement, learning is not an event—it's a way of life. Feedback is not feared—it's expected. Reflection isn't reserved for annual retreats—it happens in real time, in every meeting, project, and conversation. The culture doesn't wait for failure to demand change. It values curiosity, intentionality, and accountability as daily habits.

> "The message of the Kaizen strategy is that not a day should go by without some kind of improvement being made somewhere in the company.
>
> -Masaaki Imai

That culture starts at the top—but it doesn't live there alone. Leaders set the tone by modeling humility, asking questions, and making it safe to speak hard truths. But the real power of a learning culture is unlocked when every staff member feels responsible for improvement. When frontline staff flag broken processes. When program teams request outcome reviews before expansion. When board members ask, *"Are we doing the right thing—and doing it well?"*

In this environment, data isn't just a compliance task—it's a conversation starter. Staff aren't afraid to admit what didn't work, because failure is reframed as information. It's not about blame. It's about becoming better.

You'll recognize this kind of culture by the questions people ask:

- *"What's the goal here—and how will we know if we're achieving it?"*

- *"What's working, and how can we scale it?"*

- *"What's not working, and what do we need to change?"*

You'll also recognize it by what you don't hear: "Because we've always done it that way"—or worse, "Because that's what the funder requires." In a learning culture, compliance isn't an excuse for stagnation; it's a baseline from which thoughtful innovation begins.

Organizations that cultivate this kind of culture don't just get better results—their improvements stick because they are reinforced by values, behaviors, and expectations woven into the everyday life of the agency. Continuous improvement isn't a department. It's a posture, shared across every level, role, and responsibility.

This kind of culture doesn't emerge by accident. It's built intentionally—through hiring practices, staff development, transparent decision-making, and open dialogue. And like anything worth building, it requires ongoing care. Because just as culture can drive improvement, it can also erode it—especially in the face of leadership turnover, organizational fatigue, or shifting external pressures.

That's why protecting a learning culture is as important as building one. The systems matter. The strategies matter. But if the culture doesn't breathe curiosity, courage, and commitment, the rest will eventually break down.

BUILDING BLOCKS OF CONTINUOUS IMPROVEMENT

Continuous improvement may begin with mindset and culture, but it is sustained through practice. High-performing organizations don't just believe in getting better—they build the disciplines that make it happen. Across public, private, and nonprofit sectors, the best systems tend to invest in the same core areas: effectiveness, efficiency, workforce capacity, financial resilience, community engagement, and data-driven accountability.

These aren't just operational priorities—they're the arenas where improvement becomes measurable. Let's explore each.

Organizational Effectiveness

Excellence begins with impact. It's not enough to deliver services—we must deliver results. Effectiveness asks whether the work we're doing is producing the impact we claim to value.

That means moving beyond outputs (how many people were served) and measuring real change (what's different as a result of our work). It means tracking performance over time, comparing efforts across communities, and adjusting course when results fall short.

Effectiveness is often where real leadership is tested. It's where data collides with tradition and forces tough questions.

Earlier in my career, I helped oversee a homelessness program that provided up to a year of housing assistance while participants pursued opportunities to improve education, secure employment, or establish other resources to maintain housing after program discharge. On paper, the structure made sense – more time, more support, better outcomes. But when we reviewed the data, we found that the clients who stayed in the program longer than three months were actually less successful. They lost momentum. In contrast, those who exited in three months showed significantly higher rates of job placement and long-term housing stability.

So we changed the model. The new default was a three-month enrollment, with case-by-case extensions. We communicated this upfront, helped participants set realistic goals, and evaluated progress with integrity. The results were staggering: a 98% success rate, and over 90% housing stability six months after program exit. The lesson was clear—success is not about how long you help, but how effectively you help. And effectiveness must be verified with data.

Organizational Efficiency

Efficiency is about stewardship. It asks whether time, money, and energy are being used in ways that maximize impact and minimize waste.

In Lean methodology, one of the foundational tools is *Value Stream Mapping*—a technique used to visually analyze every step in a process to identify inefficiencies, delays, or unnecessary complexity. It's a process designed to identify waste—whether in time, effort, or materials—and align resources with what truly adds value for the customer.

ENRICHMENT

> **Efficiency doesn't mean doing less. It means removing friction so people and systems can do more - with greater purpose.**

We once worked with an organization that proudly walked us through a large packet of enrollment forms used for new customers. At first glance, the process seemed thorough. But as we walked through each page, we discovered that most of the forms weren't required by funders—and the data was already being collected in the agency's case management software. The duplication was unintentional but costly. Staff were spending unnecessary time filling out paperwork, customers were overwhelmed with redundant questions, and the agency was consuming more paper, ink, and time than needed.

By streamlining the intake process and eliminating redundant forms, the organization reclaimed valuable staff hours, reduced printing costs, and shortened the time it took to enroll and serve customers. Those savings translated into more capacity—and more people served.

Efficiency isn't about doing less—it's about doing better with what we have. The goal is not to cut for the sake of cutting, but to clear the path so people and systems can perform at their best. When we eliminate friction, we create room for focus. When we reduce redundancy, we make space for responsiveness. When we protect our resources, we position ourselves to serve more people with greater care.

Staff Growth and Capability

No system improves without people—and no people improve without support. Continuous improvement is impossible without a workforce that is skilled, empowered, and equipped to grow alongside the organization.

Developing workforce capacity means more than offering training. It's about cultivating a culture where staff are encouraged to think critically, take ownership, and lead from wherever they sit. It means cross-training team members, identifying future leaders, and creating pathways for advancement that don't rely on luck or burnout.

We worked with one organization that made a bold choice: they reserved a large portion of their administrative budget for staff development and capacity building. At first glance, it seemed excessive, but the impact was undeniable. They had low turnover and strong employee engagement. Employees—from frontline staff to senior leaders—felt valued, prepared, and included in the organization's growth. It was a strategic investment in people, and it paid off in performance, culture, and continuity.

Strong organizations also seek out input—not just in annual reviews, but continuously. Staff should be routinely asked where they feel strong and where they feel insecure. *What skills do they need to feel more confident? What training would help them serve more effectively?* These questions don't just build competence—they build trust.

Supervisors play a critical role in this process, but they shouldn't carry the burden alone. Some organizations bring in outside coaches or consultants to assess skill gaps, facilitate honest conversations, and offer professional development plans that align with both individual growth and organizational impact. When this process is done well, training doesn't feel like a checkbox. It feels like an invitation to lead.

Workforce capacity isn't just about the people we have today—it's about preparing for the people we'll need tomorrow. The question isn't just *Are our staff qualified?* It's *Are they growing? And Are we giving them the tools, voice, and support to help us grow too?*

Financial Resilience

Sustainability is more than surviving the next grant cycle. It's about building a financial foundation strong enough to weather disruption, support innovation, and grow with the community's needs.

Organizations that practice continuous improvement understand that financial stability isn't just the job of the finance team—it's a strategic concern for everyone. Just as programs must evolve to stay relevant, funding strategies must evolve to stay resilient.

This means diversifying revenue streams, building reserves, aligning spending with mission, and intentionally seeking opportunities to increase unrestricted funds. It means asking hard questions: *What percentage of our budget is tied to a single source? What programs would we lose if that funding disappeared? Are we overly dependent on restrictive grants that limit innovation or responsiveness?*

But resilience isn't just about diversity—it's about alignment. Successful organizations learn to say no to funding that pulls them off mission. They recognize that even a well-funded distraction is still a distraction. The most strategic agencies pursue funding that strengthens their core competencies, funds what works, and supports long-term vision.

MISSION ALIGNED.DATA DRIVEN.

A resilient financial model doesn't chase every dollar. It builds flexibility, honors the mission, and gives organizations room to grow, adapt, and lead—even in uncertain times.

Community Engagement

You cannot improve what you do not understand—and you cannot understand a community you don't truly listen to.

Community engagement is more than outreach. It's more than a public meeting, a survey, or a flyer. True engagement is relational, not transactional. It means inviting the community into the conversation—not just to share their needs, but to help shape the response.

> **True engagement doesn't just gather opinions - it transforms voices into direction, trust into action, and listening into leadership**

And it goes beyond those we serve directly. *Community* includes clients, yes—but also volunteers, donors, partners, advocates, and stakeholders who believe in the mission and help carry it forward. Listening to the full spectrum of voices ensures that we're not just effective in our programming—we're aligned in our purpose.

Organizations committed to continuous improvement treat the community as more than recipients of services. They recognize them as partners, co-creators, and frontline experts. They ask, *What's working for you? What's not? What do you wish we would do differently?* And most importantly—they act on what they hear.

This feedback doesn't always come through formal assessments. Sometimes it comes from hallway conversations, call center logs, social media comments, or missed appointments. Continuous improvement means building feedback loops wherever we can find them—and taking every response seriously, even when it's inconvenient.

When engagement is authentic, the result is not just better programs—it's better trust. Communities are more likely to use services they helped shape. Volunteers are more likely to stay engaged. Donors are more likely to invest. Advocates are more likely to champion the cause. In a learning culture, that feedback isn't seen as interference—it's seen as insight.

Effective organizations don't just ask the community what they think—they close the loop. They say: *"You told us this. Here's what we did."* That cycle builds legitimacy. It builds transparency. And it builds relevance—because our success depends not just on what we believe people need, but on what they tell us they need.

Continuous improvement isn't possible in isolation. Community voice—broadly and intentionally defined—ensures that we stay connected to purpose, guided by lived experience, and focused on what matters most.

Data and Accountability

Data isn't the goal. Learning is.

Too often, organizations treat data collection as a compliance task—something to satisfy a report, check a box, or meet a funding requirement. But in a culture of continuous improvement, data is not the end. It's the beginning of better questions.

What does the data tell us about who we're serving—and who we're missing? Are we reaching our intended populations? Are outcomes consistent across communities, demographics, or service types? Are the investments we're making leading to the results we promised?

Answering these questions requires more than charts and dashboards. It requires a willingness to reflect, to ask uncomfortable questions, and to act on what we find.

In Agile and Scrum, this happens through regular retrospectives—structured pauses to examine what worked, what didn't, and how to improve. In *Results Oriented Management and Accountability (ROMA)*, data is built into every phase of the process—from assessment to implementation to evaluation. In high-performing organizations, it's woven into decision-making at every level.

Accountability goes hand in hand with data. Not in the punitive sense, but in the strategic sense. A data-driven organization doesn't punish failure—it learns from it. It doesn't hide weak performance—it investigates the causes. And it doesn't collect data just to report upward—it uses it to make better decisions forward.

The strongest teams build a culture where data belongs to everyone. Program staff are trained to interpret outcome reports. Supervisors use metrics to support development, not just to monitor compliance. Leadership invites insight from across the organization—not just about what happened, but about what we can do next.

Data is only powerful if we're willing to use it—not to prove that we're right, but to discover how we can do better. That's what continuous improvement demands: curiosity, courage, and the discipline to turn numbers into knowledge—and knowledge into action.

LEADING THE CULTURE

Culture doesn't create itself. It is shaped, day by day, by what leaders model, reward, tolerate, and protect.

> "Culture doesn't create itself. It is shaped, day by day, by what leaders model, reward, tolerate, and protect."

Leadership sets the tone. Think of a champagne tower. What you pour into the top glass eventually flows into every glass below. If you pour in clarity, integrity, and purpose, those qualities cascade through the organization. But the same is true if what's poured is fear, blame, or confusion. The quality of what fills the top determines what everyone else experiences.

In organizations committed to continuous improvement, leadership is not about having all the answers—it's about creating the conditions where better answers can emerge. That starts with modeling vulnerability, curiosity, and a commitment to growth. Leaders who say *"Let's look at the data," "What did we learn from that?"* or *"How could we do this differently next time?"* signal to everyone that learning is expected—not optional, and certainly not a sign of weakness.

But leadership isn't limited to executives. Culture is built at every level. Supervisors influence how staff view feedback. Project leads set the tone for collaboration. Even informal leaders—those without a title—can reinforce the values that shape how teams respond to challenge, opportunity, or failure.

In high-functioning organizations, leadership development is part of the improvement strategy. Talented staff aren't just managed—they're mentored. Future leaders are identified early and supported as they grow. And when mistakes happen, leaders lean in—not with blame, but with clarity and support.

Protecting a learning culture is just as important as building one. Over time, even the healthiest organizations face pressure to cut corners, retreat to what's familiar, or prioritize short-term wins over long-term mission. During leadership transitions, funding shifts, or periods of rapid growth, it's easy for the values of continuous improvement to be diluted or forgotten. That's when leadership matters most.

A culture of improvement isn't built by policy. It's built by practice—by leaders who take the long view, stay grounded in purpose, and create safe spaces for reflection and honest dialogue. It's built when someone at the top says, *"We can do better,"* and everyone else knows that's not a threat—it's an invitation.

And when that invitation is accepted across the organization, excellence stops being an aspiration and starts becoming a habit.

STAYING IN MOTION

The most dangerous moment in any organization is not when things are going poorly—it's when things are going well. Success can lull us into thinking the work is done. But in a culture of continuous improvement, no milestone is mistaken for a finish line.

Excellence isn't a one-time achievement. It's a sustained refusal to settle.

That's why reflection is not a retreat activity or a year-end task. It's a daily discipline. An ongoing habit of asking:

- *Are we still becoming better?*

- *Are we still measuring what matters?*

- *Are we still responding to feedback?*

- *Are we still empowering our team to grow?*

- *Are we still listening to the people we serve—and the people who help us serve?*

- *Are we still moving toward our mission with purpose, courage, and clarity?*

When the answer to those questions is "yes," then momentum builds. Trust deepens. Impact expands. And when the answer is "no," we don't panic—we recalibrate. That's the power of a learning culture: it gives you permission to pause, assess, and adjust without shame.

Every organization, no matter how strong, faces moments of drift—moments when routines become ruts and urgency is replaced by inertia. The question isn't whether drift will happen. It's whether we'll notice it—and whether we've built the culture, the leadership, and the systems to steer back on course.

Excellence is not measured by the absence of mistakes. It's measured by the presence of intention. And organizations that commit to continuous improvement don't ask if they've arrived. They ask how they can go further—together.

FINAL THOUGHTS

Continuous improvement isn't just about fixing what's broken—it's about strengthening what already works, challenging what no longer serves, and refining what holds the most promise. It is the bridge between competence and excellence, and the fuel that sustains a mission long after initial success is achieved.

The MADD framework was never meant to be a checklist. It's a philosophy—a way of building organizations that lead with purpose, measure what matters, and grow through reflection. Enrichment is where it all comes together—where learning becomes legacy, culture becomes capacity, and excellence becomes sustainable.

Organizations that commit to continuous improvement don't do it because they're failing. They do it because they refuse to let success become a ceiling.

MISSION ALIGNED.DATA DRIVEN.

REFLECTION

Consider the following questions to determine how well you are embracing the concept of enrichment.

- **Assess:** *Are you actively and systematically looking for opportunities to improve across all areas of the organization, or just reacting to problems when they arise?*

- **Reflect:** *Where might complacency be quietly setting in?*

- **Act:** *What is one concrete step you can take in the next 30 days to reinforce a culture of continuous improvement throughout your organization?*

CHAPTER 12
LEADERSHIP COMMITMENT

LEADING THE WAY FORWARD

This book has provided you with a framework designed to challenge assumptions, shift culture, and elevate outcomes. It has explored what it means to be mission aligned, data driven, and relentlessly purposeful. But the true test of this journey begins now—because translating knowledge into leadership is where the real work begins.

Leadership in a Mission Aligned Data Driven (MADD) organization isn't about holding a title or maintaining a system. It's about carrying a responsibility—one that outlasts your tenure and transcends your comfort zone.

That responsibility doesn't belong only to executives. It belongs to anyone who influences the work, the culture, or the mission—which means it belongs to all of us. Leadership is not defined by your position on an organizational chart. It is revealed by your posture, your priorities, and your willingness to step forward when it matters most.

MISSION ALIGNED. DATA DRIVEN.

MADD leadership demands clarity in the face of noise. It requires the courage to question success, the humility to learn from failure, and the consistency to show up with purpose every single day. It asks you to guide the organization without centering yourself in it—to protect the mission, not your preferences. To steward impact, not just manage operations.

It's not always glamorous, it's not always clean, and it's rarely fast. It is, however, necessary. Because organizations don't drift toward excellence—they are led there, by people who are willing to do the quiet, intentional, often invisible work of anchoring to the mission and reaching for something better.

"Organizations don't drift toward excellence - they are led there."

Excellence is not something you achieve once and protect in a glass case. It is something you cultivate—every day, in every decision, with every step you take forward.

The framework you've just walked through is not a checklist. It is a compass. A guide for how to build organizations that reflect their deepest values, pursue their highest standards, and serve with purpose beyond personality, politics, or convenience.

Mission Aligned Data Driven leadership is not about perfection. It is about discipline. It is about refusing to drift. Refusing to hide behind tradition. Refusing to let urgency replace clarity, or routine replace impact. It is about leading with both vision and vigilance—honoring where you've come from, while refusing to let that be the limit of where you're going.

And yes, the past matters. Your history—the lessons learned, the programs built, the relationships formed—should be honored. But it cannot become a ceiling. The role of leadership is to carry forward the best of what was and let go of what no longer serves. To hold the organization's identity with reverence, but not with rigidity.

In *Leadership: Theory and Practice*[1], Peter G. Northouse explains that transformational leadership occurs when leaders engage others in ways that elevate motivation, deepen commitment to a shared vision, and raise the standard of moral purpose within an organization. That's exactly what Mission Aligned Data Driven leadership is designed to do. It centers the mission. It builds clarity around purpose. And it creates a culture where excellence is not just expected, but inspired. This kind of leadership transcends personal success and fosters the kind of alignment and growth that lasts.

This isn't a conclusion. It's a commissioning.

So lead with clarity. Lead with courage. Lead with conviction.

Because the future of your organization—and the communities it exists to serve—depends on how boldly and faithfully you carry the mission from this page to the work ahead.

Lead well. Build wisely. Protect fiercely.

And above all, leave something behind that is stronger, braver, and more beautiful than you found it.

NOTES

1. THE PURSUIT OF EXCELLENCE

1. Oxford University Press. *Oxford English Dictionary*. s.v. "excellence." Accessed June 4, 2025. https://www.oed.com/

3. THE FRAMEWORK

1. The Council for Six Sigma Certification. *Six Sigma: A Complete Step-by-Step Guide*. Buffalo, WY: Harmony Living, LLC, 2018.
2. The Council for Six Sigma Certification. *Six Sigma: A Complete Step-by-Step Guide*. Buffalo, WY: Harmony Living, LLC, 2018.
3. Liker, Jeffrey K. *The Toyota Way: 14 Management Principles from the World's Greatest Manufacturer*. McGraw-Hill, 2004.
4. Project Management Institute. *A Guide to the Project Management Body of Knowledge (PMBOK® Guide)*. 7th ed. Newtown Square, PA: Project Management Institute, 2021.
5. Beck, Kent, et al. *Manifesto for Agile Software Development*, 2001. https://agilemanifesto.org/
6. Schwaber, Ken, and Jeff Sutherland. *The Scrum Guide*, Scrum.org, 2020. https://scrumguides.org/
7. Akao, Yoji. *Hoshin Kanri: Policy Deployment for Successful TQM*. Portland, OR: Productivity Press, 1991.
8. Davenport, Thomas H., and Jeanne G. Harris. *Competing on Analytics: The New Science of Winning*.
9. University at Buffalo. "Data-Driven Decision Making (DDDM) Specialization." Coursera, 2023. https://www.coursera.org/specializations/data-driven-decision-making
10. IBM Center for The Business of Government. *Data-Driven Government: The Role of Chief Data Officers*.
11. Davenport, Thomas H., and Jeanne G. Harris. *Competing on Analytics: The New Science of Winning*.
12. McKinsey & Company. "How Nonprofits Can Tap the Potential of Data and Analytics." McKinsey & Company, 2018.
13. Stanford Social Innovation Review. "Drowning in Data." Stanford University, 2017.
14. Ohno, Taiichi. *Toyota Production System: Beyond Large-Scale Production*. Translated by Jon Miller. Portland, OR: Productivity Press, 1988.
15. Anderson, David J. *Kanban: Successful Evolutionary Change for Your Technology Business*. Blue Hole Press, 2010.

16. Burrows, Mike. *Kanban from the Inside*. Blue Hole Press, 2014.
17. Kaplan, Robert S., and David P. Norton. *The Balanced Scorecard: Translating Strategy into Action*. Boston, MA: Harvard Business School Press, 1996.
18. Niven, Paul R. *Balanced Scorecard Step-by-Step for Government and Nonprofit Agencies*. Wiley, 2003.
19. Doerr, John. *Measure What Matters: How Google, Bono, and the Gates Foundation Rock the World with OKRs*. New York: Portfolio, 2018.
20. Wodtke, Christina. *Radical Focus: Achieving Your Most Important Goals with Objectives and Key Results*. Boxes and Arrows Press, 2016.
21. Wickman, Gino. *Traction: Get a Grip on Your Business*. Dallas, TX: BenBella Books, 2012.
22. Wickman, Gino. *Get a Grip: An Entrepreneurial Fable*. BenBella Books, 2012.
23. Drucker, Peter F. *The Practice of Management*. New York: Harper & Row, 1954.
24. McChesney, Chris, Sean Covey, and Jim Huling. *The 4 Disciplines of Execution: Achieving Your Wildly Important Goals*. New York: Free Press, 2012.
25. Wootton, Simon, and Terry Horne. *Strategic Thinking: A Step-by-Step Approach to Strategy and Leadership*. 2nd ed. London: Kogan Page, 2010.
26. Sharpe, Bill, with Anthony Hodgson, Graham Leicester, Andrew Lyon, and Ioan Fazey. *Three Horizons: The Patterning of Hope*. Devon, UK: Triarchy Press, 2013.

5. IDENTITY

1. Encyclopaedia Britannica. "Poverty." *Britannica*, 2024. https://www.britannica.com/topic/poverty.
2. Maslow, A. H. "A Theory of Human Motivation." *Psychological Review* 50, no. 4 (1943): 370–396.

8. PERFORMANCE

1. Scroggins, Clay. *How to Lead in a World of Distraction: Four Simple Habits for Turning Down the Noise*. Grand Rapids, MI: Zondervan, 2019.

9. INSPECTION

1. Carter, Reginald. *The Accountable Agency: A Guide to Performance-Based Management in Human Service Organizations*. Beverly Hills, CA: SAGE Publications, 1983.
2. Frederick Richmond and Barbara Mooney. *An Introduction to Results-Oriented Management and Accountability (ROMA)*. Washington, DC: Center for Applied Management Practices, 2000.

10. REPORTING

1. Wilbur Schramm. *The Process and Effects of Mass Communication*. Urbana: University of Illinois Press, 1954.
2. Cooper, Alan. "The Long Road to Inventing Design Personas." *OneZero*. Medium, February 4, 2020. https://onezero.medium.com/in-1983-i-created-secret-weapons-for-interactive-design-d154eb8cfd58.
3. Cooper, Alan. *The Inmates Are Running the Asylum: Why High-Tech Products Drive Us Crazy and How to Restore the Sanity*. Indianapolis: Sams Publishing, 1999.

12. LEADERSHIP COMMITMENT

1. Peter G. Northouse. *Leadership: Theory and Practice*. 9th ed. Thousand Oaks, CA: SAGE Publications, 2021.

ABOUT THE AUTHOR

Shawn Howell is a nationally respected consultant, strategist, and trainer with nearly 30 years of experience helping mission-driven organizations turn insight into impact. As the founder of SA Howell, LLC, he has partnered with dozens of nonprofits across the country, guiding leaders through the complexities of strategic planning, performance management, and cultural transformation.

Before launching his consulting firm in 2017, Shawn spent nearly two decades working within the Community Action Network—a nationwide movement of agencies dedicated to alleviating poverty and improving opportunities for low-income families.

Shawn is also an experienced socioeconomic researcher, frequently engaged in studies that help organizations identify barriers and community needs, prioritize investments, and make funding decisions that advance their mission. His work equips agencies to act with confidence—aligning limited resources with the strategies most likely to create meaningful, mission-centered impact.

He holds a degree in Communication and maintains professional certifications in ROMA (Master Trainer), Six Sigma (Black Belt), AI Prompt Engineering, Data-Driven Decision-Making, Forensic Accounting, and Organizational Analytics. His unique combination of operational insight and communication skill helps organizations bridge strategy and storytelling—ensuring their plans, performance, and public messaging are aligned.

He is also an accomplished videographer, with creative work featured on Delta in-flight entertainment and the ESPN SEC Network. His production credits include collaborations on projects for Chick-fil-A, Delta Air Lines, and multiple Grammy-winning artists.

A former Head Start student and the son of a Head Start teacher, Shawn brings both personal passion and professional depth to every engagement. He lives in metro Atlanta with his wife Angela, a Registered Nurse and full-time consultant with SA Howell, LLC. Angela brings decades of leadership in healthcare, human resources, and wellness, having previously served as a Director of Nursing and Administrator of a hospice program. Together, they serve organizations nationwide and are also actively involved in their local faith community at Browns Bridge Church, part of the North Point Ministries family. They are the proud parents of three sons—Tyler, Thomas, and Andrew.

linkedin.com/in/shawn-howell-63989832

Made in the USA
Columbia, SC
01 July 2025